LOW FAT
Chinese

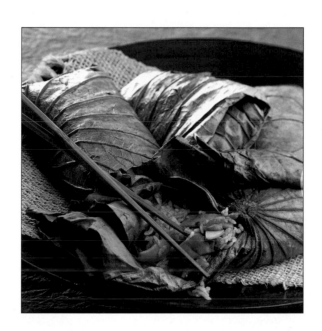

LOW FAT
Chinese

KATHY MAN

Photography by William Lingwood

southwater

This edition is published by Southwater

Southwater is an imprint of
Anness Publishing Limited
Hermes House
88-89 Blackfriars Road
London SE1 8HA
tel. 020 7401 2077
fax 020 7633 9499

Distributed in the UK by
The Manning Partnership
251-253 London Road East
Batheaston
Bath BA1 7RL
tel. 01225 852 727
fax 01225 852 852

Distributed in the USA by
Anness Publishing Inc.
27 West 20th Street
Suite 504
New York
NY 10011

Distributed in Australia by
Sandstone Publishing
Unit 1, 360 Norton Street
Leichhardt
New South Wales 2040
Australia
tel. (0061) 2 9560 7888
fax. (0061) 2 9560 7488

Southwater is an imprint of
Anness Publishing Limited
© 1998, 2000 Anness Publishing Limited

3 5 7 9 10 8 6 4

Publisher: Joanna Lorenz
Senior Cookery Editor: Linda Fraser
Designer: Brian Weldon
Indexer: Hilary Bird
Photography: William Lingwood
Food for Photography: Lucy McKelvie
Styling: Claire Louise Hunt
Production Controller: Joanna King

Previously published as Step-by-step Low Fat Chinese

Printed and bound in China

Notes
For all recipes, quantities are given in both metric and imperial measures and, where
appropriate, measures are also given in standard cups and spoons. Follow one set, but
not a mixture, because they are not interchangeable.

Standard spoon and cup measures are level.
1 tsp = 5 ml, 1 tbsp = 15 ml, 1 cup = 250 ml/8 fl oz

Australian standard tablespoons are 20 ml. Australian readers should use 3 tsp in place
of 1 tbsp for measuring small quantities of gelatine, cornflour, salt, etc.

Medium eggs are used unless otherwise stated.

CONTENTS

INTRODUCTION

Delicious Chinese dishes cooked in minutes with the minimum of fat – what could be better for the modern cook? Much Chinese food is, by its very nature, low fat. Trimmed pieces of tender meat, succulent fish and shellfish, abundant vegetables, rice and noodles; this is the stuff sensible cooks seek out. Steaming seals in all the flavour, while stir-frying is a swift and healthy method of cooking if you use a very hot non-stick pan and only a smidgen of oil.

Many of the recipes in this collection are interchangeable; for instance, the minced meat mixture used in the Crispy Turkey Balls makes an excellent alternative filling for the Stuffed Chillies and vice versa. The wontons in Seafood Wonton Soup can be filled with the mixture used for topping the Prawn Toasts with Sesame Seeds or the meat filling for the Mini Phoenix Rolls.

Familiar dishes that are traditionally deep-fried respond surprisingly well to the low fat treatment. Leaving the skin off Peking duck may sound like heresy, but when grilled marinated duck breasts are served in pancakes with the familiar sauce and fillings, the flavour is absolutely superb. Sweet-and-Sour Pork doesn't have to be deep-fried in batter; the healthier version in this collection is neither as fiddly nor as fattening, but is just as tasty as the original.

Included are some familiar dishes, such as Chicken with Cashew Nuts and Beef with Peppers and Black Bean Sauce, but also home-style favourites like Savoury Chiffon Custard. Salt "Baked" Chicken is a real winner – tender corn-fed chicken cooked in a salt crust that seals in all the delicious juices.

Most of the recipes are simplicity itself. Some of the less familiar ones may require a little more time, but the clear step-by-step pictures take any uncertainty out of the operation. The only surprise is how simple and tasty low fat Chinese cooking can be.

Flavourings and Spices

Chinese cooking is so popular that even small supermarkets tend to stock an extensive selection of flavouring ingredients.

Black bean sauce

This sauce is made from salted fermented soy beans, which have been crushed and mixed to a thick paste with flavourings. Black bean sauce is highly concentrated and is usually added to hot oil at the start of cooking to release the flavour.

Yellow bean sauce

A purée of fermented yellow beans combined with salt, flour and sugar. This is a thick, sweetish, smooth sauce and is often used in marinades.

Chillies

A wide variety of these hot members of the capsicum family is available. They are most often used for flavouring, but plump ones can be stuffed and served as a vegetable, once the fiery seeds have been removed.

Chilli oil

This reddish vegetable oil owes both its colour and spicy flavour to the chillies that have been steeped or marinated in it. Use chilli oil sparingly in cooking or as a peppery dipping sauce.

Dried shrimps

Dried, salty shrimps used as a flavouring and also as an ingredient. The shrimps are always soaked in warm water first to remove some of the salt.

They have a strong flavour, so should be used sparingly.

Five spice powder

A finely ground mixture of fennel seeds, star anise, Sichuan peppercorns, cloves and cinnamon. It has a fairly strong liquorice taste and a pungent spicy aroma and should be used sparingly. It can be used in both sweet and savoury dishes.

Garlic

This small, aromatic vegetable is one of the most important flavouring ingredients in Chinese cooking. The most common way of preparing

garlic is to peel it, then chop it finely or mince it. However, garlic is sometimes simply bruised or peeled and sliced.

Above: Some typically piquant flavourings: dried shrimps, five spice powder and liquorice-tasting whole star anise.

Ginger

Fresh root ginger is an essential flavouring ingredient in Chinese cooking. It is peeled, then sliced, shredded or minced before use. Dried ginger or ground ginger do not have the same fresh flavour and are not suitable as a substitute. Fresh root ginger freezes well. Keep a well-wrapped, peeled root in the freezer and grate it as required. It will thaw instantly.

Hoisin sauce

A thick, rich, dark sauce often used for flavouring meat and

Left: Chilli oil, sesame oil and rice vinegar enliven savoury dishes.

poultry before cooking. It is also sometimes used as one of the ingredients in a dipping sauce.

Lotus leaves

The dried leaves of the lotus plant are used as an aromatic wrapping for steamed dishes. Lotus leaves must be soaked in warm water for 30 minutes to soften them before use.

Oyster sauce

This thick, dark sauce is made from oyster juice, flour, salt and sugar. It is usually added to dishes at the end of cooking.

Rice vinegar

A colourless, slightly sweet vinegar used to add sharpness to sweet-and-sour dishes. If rice vinegar is not obtainable, white wine vinegar or cider vinegar sweetened with sugar can be used as a substitute.

Rock sugar

An aptly-named ingredient that consists of irregular lumps of amber-coloured sugar. Derived from sugar cane, rock sugar is mainly used in sweet dishes and has a caramelized flavour.

Sesame oil

This aromatic oil is made from roasted sesame seeds. Small quantities are used as an accent at the end of cooking to add flavour to a dish; in Chinese cooking it is not used for frying.

Dark soy sauce

A rich, dark sauce that is used to add both colour and flavour to many sauces and marinades. Dark soy sauce is quite salty and is often used instead of salt to season a dish.

Above (clockwise from top left): Yellow bean sauce, black bean sauce, oyster sauce, dark and light soy sauce and hoisin sauce.
Below left: Garlic, fresh root ginger and red and green, dried and fresh chillies are essential ingredients in any Chinese kitchen.
Below far left: Aromatic, dried lotus leaves are commonly soaked until soft and then used to make wrapped steamed dishes, such as Sticky Rice Parcels.

Light soy sauce

A thin, dark sauce used for flavouring many Chinese dishes and also as a table condiment. The flavour is slightly lighter and fresher than dark soy sauce, but it is a little more salty.

Star anise

A strong liquorice-tasting spice mainly used to flavour meat and poultry. The whole spice is frequently used in braised dishes so that the flavour can be released and absorbed slowly.

Seaweed, Rice and Wheat Products

All these ingredients keep well in the store cupboard or freezer, so it is worth stocking up next time you visit a Chinese supermarket.

Agar agar

A setting agent made from seaweed and mainly used in sweet jellies. Unlike gelatine, agar agar must be boiled if it is to dissolve completely, and will set firm without refrigeration.

Brown rice

This unpolished, long grain rice has a delicious nutty flavour and slightly chewy texture. It is not normally used in traditional Chinese cooking, but is included here because it has gained in popularity in recent years due to its nutritional value. Some enlightened restaurateurs now offer it either boiled or stir-fried (as in this book) as an alternative to white rice.

Above: Agar agar, a setting agent made from seaweed.
Right: various types of noodles, thick and thin, fresh and dried.

Glutinous rice

This is a short grain rice that sticks together when cooked. Glutinous rice is used in both savoury and sweet dishes and is usually soaked in water for about 2 hours before being cooked over boiling water in a large steamer lined with clean muslin or cheesecloth.

Long grain rice

Polished white rice that forms the basis of most Chinese meals. The usual method of serving rice is simply boiled but sometimes, for variety and richness, boiled rice is fried with other flavouring ingredients, such as sliced spring onions, chopped button or shiitake mushrooms, garlic, dried shrimps and eggs.

Egg noodles

Thick noodles made from flour, egg and water, these are sold fresh or dried. The noodles must be boiled before being used in fried or soup dishes, such as Seafood Soup Noodles.

Left: Rice in various forms. Although white rice (long grain or the sticky glutinous type) is traditional, brown rice has become a tasty and nutritious option in Chinese cooking.

available from most Chinese supermarkets. They should be thawed, then placed in a covered bamboo steamer or heatproof plate and steamed over boiling water in a large saucepan or wok for about 3 minutes before serving.

Wonton wrappers

Made from wheat flour, eggs and water, these small, square, wafer-thin wrappers are produced specifically for making wontons, which are essentially little minced pork dumplings encased in the wrappers and then gently poached in simmering water. The wonton wrappers are available either fresh or frozen from Chinese supermarkets.

Egg vermicelli

Made from the same ingredients as egg noodles, these are much thinner. Egg vermicelli must be pre-cooked in boiling water, according to the instructions on the packet, before being used in recipes, such as Toasted Noodles with Vegetables. In this recipe, the noodles are shallow fried in a small frying pan until they stick together to form flat toasted noodle cakes, which are then used as a base for stir-fried mixed vegetables.

Rice vermicelli

Thin, white noodles made from rice flour, these are usually sold dried. The dried noodles cook very quickly and must simply be soaked in boiling water for about 5 minutes until soft before adding to stir-fries and other dishes.

Chinese pancakes

These thin, round, white pancakes, made from wheat flour and water, are best known for eating with Peking Duck. They are sold frozen and are

Right: Bamboo steamers with Chinese pancakes and wonton wrappers, both are used to wrap foods. Wonton wrappers are traditionally filled with a minced pork stuffing and then steamed or cooked in soup. Fish and shellfish can be substituted to make a low fat version.

Vegetables and Mushrooms

Authentic ingredients make all the difference.
Look out for these at oriental markets.

Bamboo shoots

Crunchy young shoots from the
bamboo plant, these have a
delicate, but distinctive flavour.
They are available in cans, either
whole, sliced or cut into thin,
matchstick-size shreds.

Chinese mushrooms

When fresh, these are sold as
shiitake mushrooms, but the
dried version is more widely
used in Chinese cooking. Dried
Chinese mushrooms have a
more concentrated flavour. Soak
in hot water before use.

Cloud ears, Wood ears

Dried edible fungi that have a
crunchy texture; cloud ears have
a more delicate flavour than
wood ears. Once reconstituted
in water they expand to many
times their original size.

Straw mushrooms

These are grown on rice straw
and have a slippery, meaty
texture with little flavour. At
present these mushrooms are
only available canned. In
Chinese cooking, they are used
mainly for their texture.

Lotus root

A crunchy vegetable with
naturally occurring holes, lotus
root is occasionally sold fresh,
but is more frequently available
dried or frozen. When cut and
pulled apart, thread-like strands
are produced from the cut
surfaces. Also known as renkon.

Taro

A starchy tuber used in both
savoury and sweet dishes. It
looks like a hairy swede with
white flesh slightly marked by
purplish dots. The flavour and
texture resemble those of a
floury potato.

Water chestnuts

Once peeled, these black-
skinned bulbs reveal a white,
crunchy interior with a sweet
flavour. Canned, peeled water
chestnuts are available in most
supermarkets, but the fresh,
unpeeled bulb can sometimes
be bought in Chinese stores.

*Above: From top left, fresh
shiitake mushrooms, canned
straw mushrooms, dried cloud
ears and Chinese mushrooms.
Left: From top left, bamboo
shoots, the large tuber known
as taro, lotus root with its
naturally occurring holes and
water chestnuts.*

Beans and Bean Products

Packed with protein, these are essential staple ingredients that no self-respecting Chinese cook should be without.

Aduki beans

Small red beans used mainly in sweet dishes. As with most pulses, aduki beans must be soaked in water before use. They should be boiled hard for 10 minutes at the start of cooking, then simmered until soft before use.

Bean curd (tofu)

As its name suggests, this is a cheese-like product made from soya beans. Fresh bean curd is sold covered in water. It has very little flavour of its own, but readily absorbs flavourings. Bean curd is used extensively in Chinese cooking and is a good source of protein. There are several different types, including "silken" tofu and smoked tofu, but the firm variety is the one normally used by the Chinese.

Dried bean curd sticks

These are sheets of bean curd, which have been formed into sticks and dried. They are an important ingredient in Chinese vegetarian dishes. They must be soaked in hot water before being used. Bean curd sticks are usually available only in Chinese supermarkets.

Above: Aduki beans, fresh bean curd and dried bean curd sticks, protein rich components of many Chinese recipes.

Equipment

You will not need any special equipment to cook the recipes in this book. There are, however, one or two inexpensive items, such as bamboo steamers or a trivet, which are well worth buying if you don't already possess them.

Bamboo steamers

These are available in a range of sizes from Chinese supermarkets and all are quite inexpensive. Steamers of the same size will stack on top of each other and offer a novel way of presenting individual portions of steamed food. Be sure to buy the steamer lid as well to prevent water from dripping on to the food that is being cooked.

Bamboo strainer (skimmer)

This is made from twisted thin wire and is wide and flat in shape with a long bamboo handle. Useful for lifting food from stock or boiling water, they come in various sizes.

Food processor

Not a traditional Chinese utensil, but nonetheless a very useful piece of equipment which saves a lot of preparation time and effort. If you do not have one, don't worry – with patience and a sharp knife, you can often achieve the desired result. Cooked foods that require puréeing can be passed through a fine sieve if necessary.

Above: Wooden spoons and spatulas, and wire strainers or skimmers with bamboo handles are ideal for stirring, turning or lifting food during cooking.

Muslin

Clean muslin is a useful cloth for straining stock. Muslin can be washed and used over and over again; scald the muslin by pouring boiling water over it in a large, heatproof bowl.

Non-stick pan

A deep-sided non-stick frying pan is essential for low fat cooking as the special coating will help to prevent the food from sticking to the pan without the need to add lots of oil.

Roasting tin and meat rack

A small roasting tin with a metal rack is useful for roasting or grilling meats as it allows the meat to cook dry, rather than in a pool of juice. This also cuts the fat content since the fat drips away.

Sharp knives

Sharp knives are vital in Chinese cooking as many ingredients are cut or chopped into bite-size pieces. A cook's knife is necessary for chopping and cutting and a small paring knife for peeling or cutting small items. It is not necessary to buy a cleaver, as this utensil can be

Left: Useful pans for stir-frying include a non-stick frying pan with deep sides and single handed woks. Save two-handled woks for steaming.

heavy and needs getting used to if it is to be used effectively.

Trivet

A round metal trivet is very useful in the kitchen. When steaming in a wok or saucepan, stand the trivet in the pan to raise a plate or bamboo steamer above the water level.

Woks

Non-stick woks are available but tend to be fairly expensive. Unless you already have a non-stick wok, use a deep-sided non-stick frying pan for stir-frying and save your iron wok for steaming. When buying a wok, give some thought to its use. Two-handled woks are used for steaming and braising, while those with a single long handle are normally used for stir-frying (the wok is lifted and shaken with one hand while the other hand stirs the food inside).

Wok lid

The domed lid that is provided with the wok is extremely useful for steaming. It provides ample space for the steam to circulate and also allows the condensed water to slip down the sides without falling on to the food.

Wooden spoons and spatulas

When using a non-stick pan it is important to use a wooden spoon or spatula to stir the food so that the non-stick coating is neither scratched nor damaged.

Right: Bamboo steamers in different sizes, with tight-fitting lids. Several steamers can be stacked and used at once.

TECHNIQUES AND BASIC RECIPES

Preparing Prawns

While not harmful, the black thread-like vein may spoil the flavour of prawns if not removed.

1 Holding the prawn firmly in one hand, pull off the legs with the fingers of the other hand. Pull off the head.

2 Peel the shell away from the body. When you reach the tail, hold the body and firmly pull away the tail; the shell will come off with it.

3 Make a shallow cut down the centre of the curved back of the prawn. Using the knife tip, pull out and discard the black vein that runs along the length of the body.

Preparing Squid

Large or small squid are easy to prepare once you know how, and there is very little waste.

1 Holding the body of the squid in one hand, gently pull away the head and tentacles. Discard the head, then trim and reserve the tentacles.

2 Remove the transparent "quill" from inside the body of the squid, then peel off the purple skin. Rub a little salt into the squid and wash well.

3 Cut the body of the squid into rings or slit it open lengthways, score criss-cross patterns on the inside and cut it into pieces.

Five Ways of Cutting Spring Onions

In Chinese cooking, the appearance of a dish is almost as important as its taste.

1 Trim off the roots and remove any wilted ends or leaves.

2 Rings: gather the spring onions and cut straight across into fine rings.

3 Diagonal cuts: thickly slice the spring onions, holding the knife at an angle of about 60° to give uniform diamond-shaped pieces.

4 Shreds: cut the spring onions into 5 cm/2 in lengths, then slice each piece in half lengthways. Finally, cut the spring onions lengthways into fine shreds.

5 Chunks: cut the spring onions into uniform 2.5 cm/1 in pieces.

6 Tassels: cut the white part only into 6 cm/2½ in lengths. Shred one end of each piece, keeping the other end of the piece intact. Place in iced water for about 30 minutes until the shreds curl.

Cutting Carrots and Similar Vegetables

Use these techniques for other firm vegetables, such as courgettes.

1 Peel the carrots using a vegetable peeler and trim off both ends.

2 Rounds: hold the carrot with one hand and cut straight across to give thin, uniformly-sized rounds.

3 Diagonal cuts: holding the knife with the blade at an angle of about 60°, cut the carrot into thin, even diagonal slices.

4 Matchsticks: cut the carrot into thin diagonal slices (see step 3 above). Stack two or three of the slices at a time and cut them into matchsticks.

5 Roll cuts: holding one end of the carrot firmly, cut the other end off diagonally in a fairly thick slice. Roll the carrot through 180° and make another diagonal slice to make a triangular wedge. Roll and slice the rest of the carrot in the same way.

Preparing Fresh Root Ginger

Always use a very sharp knife to ensure that the pieces are an even size.

1 Bruising: lay the washed but unpeeled ginger on a board. Using the side of a large knife, a cleaver or a rolling pin, bang down hard on the ginger.

2 Peeling: trim the ginger, removing any of the knobbly pieces. Using a swivel potato peeler or a small sharp knife, peel off the skin.

3 Slicing: holding the ginger firmly with one hand, cut diagonally in thin slices.

4 Shredding: stack several thin slices of ginger on top of each other and cut carefully into fine shreds.

5 Chopping: gather the shreds together and cut across to give fine pieces, then chop repeatedly until the ginger is finely minced.

Preparing Dried Chinese Mushrooms or Cloud Ears

Dried wood ears are prepared in the same way as the cloud ears pictured here.

1 Soak mushrooms or cloud ears in hot water for 30 minutes or until softened. Rinse thoroughly.

2 Remove and discard the stalks from the soaked mushrooms and use the caps whole, sliced or chopped.

3 Cut the soaked cloud ears into small pieces, discarding the tough base.

Vegetable Stock

Use this light, but flavoursome stock for cooking rice and noodles, as well as for soup.

Makes about 1.2 litres/2 pints/5 cups

INGREDIENTS
3 carrots
2 courgettes
2 leeks
1 celery stick
1 large onion
10 black peppercorns
1.2 litres/2 pints/5 cups cold water

1 Cut the carrot into chunks. Slice the courgettes, leeks, celery and onion.

2 Place all the vegetables in a large saucepan with the peppercorns and water. Bring to the boil, lower the heat, cover and simmer for 15 minutes.

3 Allow the stock to cool before straining through a sieve lined with muslin. The stock can be stored in the fridge for up to 3 days or frozen for about 3 weeks.

Fish Stock

Make shellfish stock in the same way using an equivalent amount of prawn shells and heads.

Makes about 1.75 litres/3 pints/7½ cups

INGREDIENTS
1 onion
2 leeks
2 carrots
1.5 kg/3–3½ lb fish heads and bones
5 black peppercorns
1.75 litre/3 pints/7½ cups cold water

1 Cut the onion into quarters, slice the leeks and cut the carrots into chunks.

2 Place all the vegetables and the fish heads and bones in a large saucepan with the peppercorns and water. Bring to the boil. Skim off any scum which rises to the surface, then lower the heat, cover and simmer for 15 minutes.

3 Allow the stock to cool completely. Strain through a sieve lined with muslin before use. The stock can be stored in the fridge for 2–3 days or frozen for 2–3 weeks.

Chicken Stock

This versatile stock is an essential ingredient in every Chinese kitchen.

Makes about 1.5 litres/2½ pints/6¼ cups

INGREDIENTS
3 chicken carcasses
2 onions, quartered
3 carrots, cut into large chunks
5 cm/2 in piece of fresh root
    ginger, bruised
10 black peppercorns
1.75 litres/3 pints/7½ cups cold
    water

1 Using a pair of poultry shears, cut the chicken carcasses into small pieces. Place them in a large saucepan. Add the onions, carrots, ginger, peppercorns and water and bring to the boil.

2 Boil for 5 minutes, skimming off any scum that rises to the surface. Lower the heat, cover and simmer for 1 hour.

3 Allow the stock to cool. Strain through a sieve lined with muslin. The stock can be stored in the fridge for 2–3 days or frozen for 2–3 weeks. Skim off any hardened fat from the surface of the stock before use.

Beef Stock

Browning the beef bones in the oven first creates a richly flavoured stock.

Makes about 1.2 litres/2 pints/5 cups

INGREDIENTS
2.25 kg/5 lb beef shin bones, broken
    into small pieces
4 carrots, cut into large chunks
2 onions, quartered
2 celery sticks, cut into large pieces
5 garlic cloves, crushed
10 black peppercorns
1.75 litres/3 pints/7½ cups cold
    water

1 Preheat the oven to 190°C/375°F/ Gas 5. Spread out the beef bones in a large roasting tin. Add the prepared carrots, onions, celery and garlic and roast for about 25 minutes.

2 Using a slotted spoon or tongs, transfer the bones and vegetables to a large saucepan, leaving behind any fat in the roasting tin. Add the peppercorns.

3 Pour in the water and bring to the boil. Boil for 5 minutes, skimming off any scum which rises to the surface of the liquid, then lower the heat, cover and simmer for 2 hours. The stock can be stored in the fridge for 2–3 days or frozen for 2–3 weeks. Skim off any hardened fat from the surface of the stock before use.

Seafood Wonton Soup

This is a variation on the popular wonton soup that is traditionally prepared using pork.

Serves 4

INGREDIENTS

50 g/2 oz raw tiger prawns
50 g/2 oz queen scallops
75 g/3 oz skinless cod
    fillet, roughly chopped
15 ml/1 tbsp finely chopped chives
5 ml/1 tsp dry sherry
1 small egg white, lightly beaten
2.5 ml/½ tsp sesame oil
1.5 ml/¼ tsp salt
large pinch of ground white pepper
900 ml/1½ pints/3¾ cups fish stock
20 wonton wrappers
2 cos lettuce leaves, shredded
fresh coriander leaves and garlic
    chives, to garnish

cod fillet

wonton
wrappers

cos
lettuce

fresh
coriander   sherry   prawns

egg   sesame oil

scallops   chives

fish stock

NUTRITIONAL NOTES
PER PORTION:

ENERGY 115 Kcals/480 KJ **FAT** 5.2 g
SATURATED FAT 0.6 g
CHOLESTEROL 109 mg

1 Peel and devein the prawns. Rinse them well, pat them dry on kitchen paper and cut them into small pieces.

2 Rinse the scallops. Pat them dry, using kitchen paper. Chop them into small pieces the same size as the prawns.

3 Place the cod in a food processor and process until a paste is formed. Scrape into a bowl and stir in the prawns, scallops, chives, sherry, egg white, sesame oil, salt and pepper. Mix thoroughly, cover and leave in a cool place to marinate for 20 minutes.

4 Heat the fish stock gently in a saucepan. Make the wontons. Place a teaspoonful of the seafood filling in the centre of a wonton wrapper, then bring the corners together to meet at the top. Twist them together to enclose the filling. Fill the remaining wonton wrappers in the same way.

5 Bring a large saucepan of water to the boil. Drop in the wontons. When the water returns to the boil, lower the heat and simmer gently for 5 minutes or until the wontons float to the surface. Drain the wontons and divide them among four heated soup bowls.

6 Add a portion of lettuce to each bowl. Bring the fish stock to the boil. Ladle it into each bowl, garnish each portion with coriander leaves and garlic chives and serve immediately.

COOK'S TIP
The filled wonton wrappers can be made ahead, then frozen for several weeks and cooked straight from the freezer.

Hot-and-Sour Soup

This spicy, warming soup really whets the appetite and is the perfect introduction to a simple Chinese meal.

Serves 4

INGREDIENTS

10 g/¼ oz dried cloud ears
8 fresh shiitake mushrooms
75 g/3 oz bean curd (tofu)
50 g/2 oz/½ cup sliced, drained, canned bamboo shoots
900 ml/1½ pints/3¾ cups vegetable stock
15 ml/1 tbsp caster sugar
45 ml/3 tbsp rice vinegar
15 ml/1 tbsp light soy sauce
1.5 ml/¼ tsp chilli oil
2.5 ml/½ tsp salt
large pinch of ground white pepper
15 ml/1 tbsp cornflour
15 ml/1 tbsp cold water
1 egg white
5 ml/1 tsp sesame oil
2 spring onions, cut into fine rings

1 Soak the cloud ears in hot water for 30 minutes or until soft. Drain, trim off and discard the hard base from each and chop the cloud ears roughly.

2 Remove and discard the stalks from the shiitake mushrooms. Cut the caps into thin strips. Cut the bean curd into 1 cm/½ in cubes and shred the bamboo shoots finely.

bean curd

bamboo shoots

sugar

egg

soy sauce

sesame oil

cloud ears

shiitake mushrooms

spring onions

vegetable stock

cornflour

chilli oil

rice vinegar

NUTRITIONAL NOTES
PER PORTION:

ENERGY 136 Kcals/571 KJ **FAT** 3 g
SATURATED FAT 0.35 g
CHOLESTEROL 0 mg

3 Place the stock, mushrooms, bean curd, bamboo shoots and cloud ears in a large saucepan. Bring the stock to the boil, lower the heat and simmer for about 5 minutes.

4 Stir in the sugar, vinegar, soy sauce, chilli oil, salt and pepper. Mix the cornflour to a paste with the water. Add the mixture to the soup, stirring constantly until it thickens slightly.

COOK'S TIP
To transform this tasty soup into a nutritious light meal, simply add extra mushrooms, bean curd and bamboo shoots.

5 Lightly beat the egg white, then pour it slowly into the soup in a steady stream, stirring constantly. Cook, stirring, until the egg white changes colour.

6 Add the sesame oil just before serving. Ladle into heated bowls and top each portion with spring onion rings.

Tomato and Beef Soup

Fresh tomatoes and spring onions give this light beef broth a superb flavour.

Serves 4

INGREDIENTS

75 g/3 oz rump steak, trimmed of fat
900 ml/1½ pints/3¾ cups beef stock
30 ml/2 tbsp tomato purée
6 tomatoes, halved, seeded
    and chopped
10 ml/2 tsp caster sugar
15 ml/1 tbsp cornflour
15 ml/1 tbsp cold water
1 egg white
2.5 ml/½ tsp sesame oil
2 spring onions, finely shredded
salt and ground black pepper

tomato purée

rump steak

caster sugar

beef stock

egg

tomatoes

cornflour

sesame oil

spring onions

NUTRITIONAL NOTES
PER PORTION:

ENERGY 77 Kcals/327 KJ **FAT** 1.8 g
SATURATED FAT 0.5 g
CHOLESTEROL 11 mg

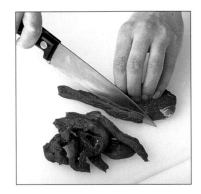

1 Cut the beef into thin strips and place it in a saucepan. Pour over boiling water to cover. Cook for 2 minutes, then drain thoroughly and set aside.

2 Bring the stock to the boil in a clean pan. Stir in the tomato purée, then the tomatoes and sugar. Add the beef strips, allow the stock to boil again, then lower the heat and simmer for 2 minutes.

COOK'S TIP
Try the soup topped with thin strips of fresh basil instead of spring onions for a more Mediterranean taste.

3 Mix the cornflour to a paste with the water. Add the mixture to the soup, stirring constantly until it thickens slightly. Lightly beat the egg white in a cup.

4 Pour the egg white into the soup in a steady stream, stirring all the time. As soon as the egg white changes colour, add salt and pepper, stir the soup and pour it into heated bowls. Drizzle each portion with a few drops of sesame oil, sprinkle with the spring onions and serve.

Prawn Toasts with Sesame Seeds

This healthy version of the ever-popular starter has lost none of its classic crunch and taste.

Serves 4–6

INGREDIENTS
6 slices medium-cut white bread, crusts removed
225 g/8 oz raw tiger prawns, peeled and deveined
50 g/2 oz/⅓ cup drained, canned water chestnuts
1 egg white
5 ml/1 tsp sesame oil
2.5 ml/½ tsp salt
2 spring onions, finely chopped
10 ml/2 tsp dry sherry
15 ml/1 tbsp sesame seeds, toasted (see Cook's Tip)
shredded spring onion, to garnish

sherry

bread

prawns

water chestnuts

egg

sesame seeds

sesame oil

spring onions

COOK'S TIP

To toast sesame seeds, put them in a dry frying pan and place over a medium heat until the seeds change colour. Shake the pan constantly to prevent them from burning.

1 Preheat the oven to 120°C/250°F/Gas ½. Cut each slice of bread into four triangles. Spread out on a baking sheet and bake for 25 minutes or until crisp.

2 Meanwhile, put the prawns in a food processor with the water chestnuts, egg white, sesame oil and salt. Process until a coarse purée is formed.

NUTRITIONAL NOTES
Per portion:

ENERGY 214Kcals/907 KJ **FAT** 4.5 g
SATURATED FAT 0.7 g
CHOLESTEROL 109 mg

3 Scrape the mixture into a bowl, stir in the chopped spring onions and sherry and marinate for 10 minutes.

4 Remove the toast from the oven and raise the temperature to 200°C/400°F/Gas 6. Spread the prawn mixture on the toast, sprinkle with sesame seeds and bake for 12 minutes. Garnish with spring onion and serve hot or warm.

Crispy Turkey Balls

Turkey is not traditionally used in Chinese cooking but makes a good alternative to chicken.

Serves 4–6

INGREDIENTS
4 thin slices of white bread, crusts removed
5 ml/1 tsp olive oil
225 g/8 oz skinless, boneless turkey meat, roughly chopped
50 g/2 oz/⅓ cup drained, canned water chestnuts
2 fresh red chillies, seeded and roughly chopped
1 egg white
10 g/¼ oz/¼ cup fresh coriander leaves
5 ml/1 tsp cornflour
2.5 ml/½ tsp salt
1.5 ml/¼ tsp ground white pepper
30 ml/2 tbsp light soy sauce
5 ml/1 tsp caster sugar
30 ml/2 tbsp rice vinegar
2.5 ml/½ tsp chilli oil
shredded red chillies and fresh coriander sprigs, to garnish

bread *turkey*

chillies *water chestnuts*

cornflour *chilli oil* *caster sugar*

egg *soy sauce* *rice vinegar*

VARIATION
Chicken or pork can be used instead of turkey, with equally delicious results.

1 Preheat the oven to 120°C/250°F/Gas ½. Brush the bread slices lightly with olive oil and cut them into 5 mm/¼ in cubes. Spread over a baking sheet and bake for 15 minutes until dry and crisp.

2 Meanwhile, mix together the turkey meat, water chestnuts and chillies in a food processor. Process until a coarse paste is formed.

3 Add the egg white, coriander leaves, cornflour, salt and pepper. Pour in half the soy sauce and process for about 30 seconds. Scrape into a bowl, cover and leave in a cool place for 20 minutes.

4 Remove the toasted bread cubes from the oven and set them aside. Raise the oven temperature to 200°C/400°F/Gas 6. With dampened hands, divide the turkey mixture into 12 portions and form into balls.

5 Roughly crush the toasted bread cubes, then transfer to a plate. Roll each ball in turn over the toasted crumbs until coated. Place on a baking sheet and bake for about 20 minutes or until the coating is brown and the turkey filling has cooked through.

6 In a small bowl, mix the remaining soy sauce with the caster sugar, rice vinegar and chilli oil. Serve the sauce with the turkey balls, garnished with shredded chillies and coriander sprigs.

NUTRITIONAL NOTES
PER PORTION:

ENERGY 183 Kcals/778 KJ **FAT** 2.8 g
SATURATED FAT 0.5 g
CHOLESTEROL 3.2 mg

Mussels in Black Bean Sauce

The large green-shelled mussels from New Zealand are perfect for this delicious dish. Buy the cooked mussels on the half shell.

Serves 4

INGREDIENTS

15 ml/1 tbsp vegetable oil
2.5 cm/1 in piece of fresh root
 ginger, finely chopped
2 garlic cloves, finely chopped
1 fresh red chilli, seeded
 and chopped
15 ml/1 tbsp black bean sauce
15 ml/1 tbsp dry sherry
5 ml/1 tsp caster sugar
5 ml/1 tsp sesame oil
10 ml/2 tsp dark soy sauce
20 cooked New Zealand green-
 shelled mussels
2 spring onions, 1 shredded and
 1 cut into fine rings

garlic
ginger
chilli
mussels
black bean sauce
sherry
caster sugar
soy sauce
sesame oil
vegetable oil
spring onions

NUTRITIONAL NOTES
PER PORTION:

ENERGY 90 Kcals/514 KJ **FAT** 4.4 g
SATURATED FAT 0.6 g
CHOLESTEROL 14.2 mg

1 Heat the vegetable oil in a small frying pan. Fry the ginger, garlic and chilli with the black bean sauce for a few seconds, then add the sherry and caster sugar and cook for 30 seconds more.

2 Remove the sauce from the heat and stir in the sesame oil and soy sauce. Mix thoroughly.

COOK'S TIP
Large scallops in their shells can be cooked in the same way. Do not overcook the shellfish.

3 Have ready a saucepan with about 5 cm/2 in of boiling water and a heatproof plate that will fit neatly inside it. Place the mussels in a single layer on the plate. Spoon over the sauce.

4 Sprinkle the spring onions over the mussels, cover the plate tightly with foil and place it in the pan on a metal trivet. Steam over a high heat for about 10 minutes or until the mussels have heated through. Serve immediately.

Stuffed Chillies

This pretty dish is not as fiery as you might expect. Do give it a try.

Serves 4–6

INGREDIENTS
10 fat fresh green chillies
115 g/4 oz lean pork,
    roughly chopped
75 g/3 oz raw tiger prawns, peeled
    and deveined
15 g/½ oz/½ cup fresh
    coriander leaves
5 ml/1 tsp cornflour
10 ml/2 tsp dry sherry
10 ml/2 tsp soy sauce
5 ml/1 tsp sesame oil
2.5 ml/½ tsp salt
15 ml/1 tbsp cold water
1 fresh red and 1 fresh green chilli,
    seeded and sliced into rings, and
    cooked peas, to garnish

prawns

chillies

pork

coriander

sherry

sesame oil

soy sauce

cornflour

NUTRITIONAL NOTES
PER PORTION:

ENERGY 72 Kcals/302 KJ FAT 2.3 g
SATURATED FAT 0.55 g
CHOLESTEROL 54.8 mg

COOK'S TIP
If you prefer a slightly hotter taste, stuff fresh hot red chillies as well as the green ones.

1 Cut the chillies in half lengthways, keeping the stalk. Scrape out and discard the seeds and set the chillies aside.

2 Mix together the pork, prawns and coriander leaves in a food processor. Process until smooth. Scrape into a bowl and mix in the cornflour, sherry, soy sauce, sesame oil, salt and water; cover and leave to marinate for 10 minutes.

3 Fill each half chilli with some of the meat mixture. Have ready a steamer or a heatproof plate and a pan with about 5 cm/2 in boiling water.

4 Place the stuffed chillies in the steamer or on a plate, meat side up, and cover with a lid or foil. Steam steadily for 15 minutes or until the meat filling is cooked. Serve immediately, garnished with the chilli rings and peas.

Mini Phoenix Rolls

These rolls are ideal as an easy starter and can be served hot or cold.

Serves 4

INGREDIENTS

2 large eggs, plus 1 egg white
75 ml/5 tbsp cold water
5 ml/1 tsp vegetable oil
175 g/6 oz lean pork, diced
75 g/3 oz/½ cup drained, canned
    water chestnuts
5 cm/2 in piece of fresh root
    ginger, grated
4 dried Chinese mushrooms, soaked
    in hot water until soft
15 ml/1 tbsp dry sherry
1.5 ml/¼ tsp salt
large pinch of ground white pepper
30 ml/2 tbsp rice vinegar
2.5 ml/½ tsp caster sugar
fresh coriander or flat leaf parsley,
    to garnish

root ginger

pork

dry sherry

vegetable oil

water chestnuts

Chinese mushrooms

rice vinegar

eggs

caster sugar

NUTRITIONAL NOTES

Per portion:

ENERGY 156 Kcals/703 KJ FAT 6 g
SATURATED FAT 1.6 g
CHOLESTEROL 144 mg

1 Lightly beat the 2 whole eggs with 45 ml/3 tbsp of the water. Heat a 20 cm/8 in non-stick omelette pan and brush with a little of the oil. Pour in a quarter of the egg mixture, swirling the pan to coat the base lightly. Cook the omelette until the top is set. Slide it on to a plate and make three more omelettes in the same way.

2 Mix the pork and water chestnuts in a food processor. Add 5 ml/1 tsp of the root ginger. Drain the mushrooms, chop the caps roughly and add these to the mixture. Process until smooth.

3 Scrape the pork paste into a bowl. Stir in the egg white, sherry, remaining water, salt and pepper. Mix thoroughly, cover and leave in cool place for about 15 minutes.

4 Have ready a saucepan with about 5 cm/2 in boiling water and a large heatproof plate that will fit inside it on a metal trivet. Divide the pork mixture among the omelettes and spread into a large square shape in the centre of each of the omelettes.

5 Bring the sides of each omelette over the filling and roll up from the bottom to the top. Arrange the rolls on the plate. Cover the plate tightly with foil and place it in the pan on the trivet. Steam over a high heat for 15 minutes.

COOK'S TIP
These rolls can be prepared a day in advance and steamed just before serving.

6 Make a dipping sauce by mixing the remaining ginger with the rice vinegar and sugar in a small dish. Cut the rolls diagonally in 1 cm/½ in slices, garnish with the coriander or flat leaf parsley leaves and serve with the sauce.

Chicken and Vegetable Bundles

This popular and delicious dim sum is extremely easy to prepare in your own kitchen.

Serves 4

INGREDIENTS
4 skinless, boneless chicken thighs
5 ml/1 tsp cornflour
10 ml/2 tsp dry sherry
30 ml/2 tbsp light soy sauce
2.5 ml/½ tsp salt
large pinch of ground white pepper
4 fresh shiitake mushrooms
50 g/2 oz/½ cup sliced, drained, canned bamboo shoots
1 small carrot
1 small courgette
1 leek, trimmed
1.5 ml/¼ tsp sesame oil

1 Remove any fat from the chicken thighs and cut each lengthways into eight strips. Place the strips in a bowl.

2 Add the cornflour, sherry and half the soy sauce to the chicken. Stir in the salt and pepper and mix well. Cover and marinate for 10 minutes.

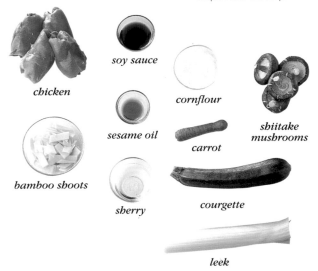

soy sauce

cornflour

chicken

shiitake mushrooms

sesame oil

carrot

bamboo shoots

sherry

courgette

leek

3 Remove and discard the mushroom stalks, then cut each mushroom cap in half (or in slices if very large). Cut the carrot and courgette into eight batons, each about 5 cm/2 in long, then mix the mushroom halves and bamboo shoots together.

4 Bring a small saucepan of water to the boil. Add the leek and blanch until soft. Drain thoroughly, then slit the leek down its length. Separate each layer to give eight long strips.

NUTRITIONAL NOTES
PER PORTION:
ENERGY 113 Kcals/475 KJ **FAT** 2.1 g
SATURATED FAT 0.5 g
CHOLESTEROL 52.5 mg

5 Divide the marinated chicken into eight portions. Do the same with the vegetables. Wrap each strip of leek around a portion of chicken and vegetables to make eight neat bundles. Have ready a saucepan with about 5 cm/2 in boiling water and a steamer or a heatproof plate that will fit inside it on a metal trivet.

6 Place the chicken and vegetable bundles in the steamer or on the plate. Place in the pan, cover and steam over a high heat for 12–15 minutes or until the filling is cooked. Meanwhile, mix the remaining soy sauce with the sesame oil and use as a sauce for the bundles.

Grey Mullet with Pork

This unusual combination makes a spectacular main dish with little effort.

Serves 4

INGREDIENTS
1 grey mullet, about 900 g/2 lb, gutted and cleaned
50 g/2 oz lean pork
3 dried Chinese mushrooms, soaked in hot water until soft
2.5 ml/½ tsp cornflour
30 ml/2 tbsp light soy sauce
15 ml/1 tbsp vegetable oil
15 ml/1 tbsp finely shredded fresh root ginger
15 ml/1 tbsp shredded spring onion
salt and ground black pepper
rice, to serve
sliced spring onion, to garnish

dried Chinese mushrooms

pork

cornflour soy sauce

grey mullet

root ginger

spring onion

vegetable oil

NUTRITIONAL NOTES
PER PORTION:

ENERGY 256 Kcals/1213 KJ **FAT** 10 g
SATURATED FAT 2.3 g
CHOLESTEROL 62 mg

COOK'S TIP
If the fish is too big to fit into the steamer whole, simply cut the fish in half for cooking, then reassemble it to serve.

1 Make four diagonal cuts on either side of the fish and rub with a little salt; place the fish on a large shallow heatproof serving dish.

2 Cut the pork into thin strips. Place in a bowl. Drain the soaked mushrooms, remove and discard the stalks and slice the caps thinly.

3 Add the mushrooms to the pork, with the cornflour and half the soy sauce. Stir in 5 ml/1 tsp of the oil and a generous grinding of black pepper. Arrange the pork mixture along the length of the fish. Scatter the ginger shreds over the top.

4 Cover the fish loosely with foil. Have ready a large saucepan or roasting tin with about 5 cm/2 in boiling water, which is big enough to fit the heatproof dish inside it on a metal trivet. Place the dish in the pan or roasting tin, cover and steam over a high heat for 15 minutes.

5 Test the fish by pressing the flesh gently. If it comes away from the bone with a slight resistance, the fish is cooked. Carefully pour away any excess liquid from the dish.

6 Heat the remaining oil in a small pan. When it is hot, fry the shredded spring onion for a few seconds, then pour it over the fish, taking great care as it will splatter. Drizzle with the remaining soy sauce, garnish with sliced spring onion and serve immediately with rice.

Three Sea Flavours Stir-fry

This delectable seafood combination is enhanced by the use of fresh root ginger and spring onions.

Serves 4

INGREDIENTS

4 large scallops, with the corals
225 g/8 oz firm white fish fillet, such as monkfish or cod
115 g/4 oz raw tiger prawns
300 ml/½ pint/1¼ cups fish stock
15 ml/1 tbsp vegetable oil
2 garlic cloves, coarsely chopped
5 cm/2 in piece of fresh root ginger, thinly sliced
8 spring onions, cut into 4 cm/ 1½ in pieces
30 ml/2 tbsp dry white wine
5 ml/1 tsp cornflour
15 ml/1 tbsp cold water
salt and ground white pepper
noodles or rice, to serve

fish stock
wine
garlic
prawns
root ginger
vegetable oil
fish fillet
cornflour
scallops
spring onions

NUTRITIONAL NOTES

PER PORTION:

ENERGY 189 Kcals/937 KJ **FAT** 4.6 g
SATURATED FAT 0.7 g
CHOLESTEROL 96.7 mg

COOK'S TIP
Do not overcook the seafood or it will become rubbery.

1 Separate the corals and slice each scallop in half horizontally. Cut the fish fillet into bite-size chunks. Peel and devein the prawns.

2 Bring the fish stock to the boil in a saucepan. Add the seafood, lower the heat and poach gently for 1–2 minutes until the fish, scallops and corals are just firm and the prawns have turned pink. Drain the seafood, reserving about 60 ml/4 tbsp of the stock.

3 Heat the oil in a non-stick frying pan or wok over a high heat until very hot. Stir-fry the garlic, ginger and spring onions for a few seconds.

4 Add the seafood and wine. Stir-fry for 1 minute, then add the reserved stock and simmer for 2 minutes.

5 Mix the cornflour to a paste with the water. Add the mixture to the pan or wok and cook, stirring gently just until the sauce thickens.

6 Season the stir-fry with salt and pepper to taste. Serve at once, with noodles or rice.

Stir-fried Prawns with Mangetouts

Prawns and mangetouts make a very pretty dish, which needs no embellishment.

Serves 4

INGREDIENTS

300 ml/½ pint/1¼ cups fish stock
350 g/12 oz raw tiger prawns,
    peeled and deveined
15 ml/1 tbsp vegetable oil
1 garlic clove, finely chopped
225 g/8 oz/2 cups mangetouts
1.5 ml/¼ tsp salt
15 ml/1 tbsp dry sherry
15 ml/1 tbsp oyster sauce
5 ml/1 tsp cornflour
5 ml/1 tsp caster sugar
15 ml/1 tbsp cold water
1.5 ml/¼ tsp sesame oil

mangetouts   *prawns*

sherry   *cornflour*   *sugar*

oyster sauce   *sesame oil*

garlic

fish stock

NUTRITIONAL NOTES
PER PORTION:

ENERGY 132 Kcals/693 KJ **FAT** 3.8 g
SATURATED FAT 0.4 g
CHOLESTEROL 170 mg

1 Bring the fish stock to the boil in a frying pan. Add the prawns. Cook gently for 2 minutes until the prawns have turned pink, then drain and set aside.

2 Heat the vegetable oil in a non-stick frying pan or wok. Add the chopped garlic and cook for a few seconds, then add the mangetouts. Sprinkle with the salt. Stir-fry for 1 minute.

3 Add the prawns and sherry to the pan or wok. Stir-fry for a few seconds, then add the oyster sauce.

4 Mix the cornflour and sugar to a paste with the water. Add the mixture to the pan and cook, stirring constantly, until the sauce thickens slightly. Drizzle with the sesame oil and serve.

Asparagus with Crabmeat Sauce

The subtle flavour of fresh asparagus is enhanced by the equally delicate taste of the crabmeat in this classic dish.

Serves 4

INGREDIENTS

450 g/1 lb asparagus, trimmed
15 ml/1 tbsp vegetable oil
4 thin slices of fresh root ginger
2 garlic cloves, finely chopped
115 g/4 oz/²⁄₃ cup fresh or thawed
    frozen white crabmeat
5 ml/1 tsp dry sherry
150 ml/¼ pint/²⁄₃ cup semi-
    skimmed milk
15 ml/1 tbsp cornflour
45 ml/3 tbsp cold water
salt and ground white pepper
1 spring onion, thinly shredded,
    to garnish

garlic

root ginger

sherry

asparagus

vegetable oil

semi-skimmed milk

crabmeat

cornflour

spring onion

NUTRITIONAL NOTES
PER PORTION:

ENERGY 109 Kcals/594 KJ **FAT** 4.1 g
SATURATED FAT 0.8 g
CHOLESTEROL 23 mg

1 Bring a large pan of lightly salted water to the boil. Poach the asparagus for about 5 minutes until just crisp-tender. Drain well and keep hot in a shallow serving dish.

2 Heat the oil in a non-stick frying pan or wok. Cook the ginger and garlic for 1 minute to release their flavour, then lift them out with a slotted spoon and discard them.

3 Add the crabmeat, sherry and milk to the flavoured oil and cook, stirring often, for 2 minutes.

4 In a small bowl, mix the cornflour to a paste with the water and add to the pan. Cook, stirring constantly, until the sauce is thick and creamy. Season to taste with salt and pepper, spoon over the asparagus, garnish with shreds of spring onion and serve.

Gong Boa Prawns

A pleasantly spicy sweet-and-sour dish that takes only minutes to make.

Serves 4

INGREDIENTS

350 g/12 oz raw tiger prawns
½ cucumber, about 75 g/3 oz
300 ml/½ pint/1¼ cups fish stock
15 ml/1 tbsp vegetable oil
2.5 ml/½ tsp crushed dried chillies
½ green pepper, seeded and cut
   into 2.5 cm/1 in strips
1 small carrot, thinly sliced
30 ml/2 tbsp tomato ketchup
45 ml/3 tbsp rice vinegar
15 ml/1 tbsp caster sugar
150 ml/¼ pint/⅔ cup vegetable
   stock
50 g/2 oz/½ cup drained canned
   pineapple chunks
10 ml/2 tsp cornflour
15 ml/1 tbsp cold water
salt

1 Peel and devein the prawns. Rub them gently with 2.5 ml/½ tsp salt; leave them for a few minutes and then wash and dry thoroughly.

2 Using a narrow peeler or canelle knife, pare strips of skin off the cucumber to give a stripy effect. Cut the cucumber in half lengthways and scoop out the seeds with a teaspoon. Cut the flesh into 5 mm/¼ in crescents.

3 Bring the fish stock to the boil in a saucepan. Add the prawns, lower the heat and poach the prawns for about 2 minutes until they turn pink, then drain and set aside.

green pepper
prawns
cucumber
crushed dried chillies
ketchup
caster sugar

vegetable stock
pineapple chunks
rice vinegar
fish stock

cornflour
carrot

4 Heat the oil in a non-stick frying pan or wok over a high heat. Fry the chillies for a few seconds, then add the pepper strips and carrot slices and stir-fry for 1 minute.

5 Mix together the tomato ketchup, vinegar, sugar and vegetable stock, with 1.5 ml/¼ tsp salt. Pour into the pan and cook for 3 minutes more.

NUTRITIONAL NOTES

PER PORTION:

ENERGY 145 Kcals/750 KJ **FAT** 3.9 g
SATURATED FAT 0.4 g
CHOLESTEROL 170 mg

COOK'S TIP
Omit the chillies if you like, or increase the quantity for a spicier dish.

6 Add the prawns, cucumber and pineapple and cook for 2 minutes more. Mix the cornflour to a paste with the water. Add the mixture to the pan and cook, stirring constantly, until the sauce thickens. Serve at once.

Spicy Squid Salad

This tasty, colourful salad is a refreshing way of serving succulent squid.

Serves 4

INGREDIENTS

450 g/1 lb squid
300 ml/½ pint/1¼ cups fish stock
175 g/6 oz green beans, trimmed
    and halved
45 ml/3 tbsp fresh coriander leaves
10 ml/2 tsp caster sugar
30 ml/2 tbsp rice vinegar
5 ml/1 tsp sesame oil
15 ml/1 tbsp light soy sauce
15 ml/1 tbsp vegetable oil
2 garlic cloves, finely chopped
10 ml/2 tbsp finely chopped fresh
    root ginger
1 fresh chilli, seeded and chopped
salt

fish stock
green beans
coriander
caster sugar
squid
rice vinegar
sesame oil
vegetable oil
soy sauce
garlic
chilli
root ginger

NUTRITIONAL NOTES
Per portion:

ENERGY 67 Kcals/415 KJ **FAT** 4.3 g
SATURATED FAT 0.5 g
CHOLESTEROL 0 mg

COOK'S TIP
If you hold your knife at an angle when scoring the squid there is less of a risk of cutting right through it.

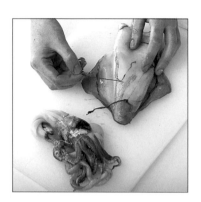

1 Prepare the squid. Holding the body in one hand, gently pull away the head and tentacles. Discard the head; trim and reserve the tentacles. Remove the transparent "quill" from inside the body of the squid and peel off the purplish skin on the outside.

2 Cut the body of the squid open lengthways and wash thoroughly. Score criss-cross patterns on the inside, taking care not to cut through the squid, then cut into 7.5 × 5 cm/3 × 2 in pieces.

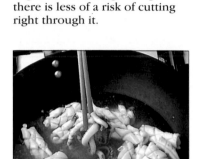

3 Bring the fish stock to the boil in a wok or saucepan. Add all the squid pieces, then lower the heat and cook for about 2 minutes until they are tender and have curled. Drain.

4 In a separate pan of lightly salted boiling water, cook the beans until crisp-tender. Drain, refresh under cold water, then drain again. Mix the squid and beans in a serving bowl.

5 In a bowl or jug, mix the coriander leaves, sugar, rice vinegar, sesame oil and soy sauce. Pour the mixture over the squid and beans.

6 Heat the vegetable oil in a wok or small pan until very hot. Stir-fry the garlic, ginger and chilli for a few seconds, then pour the dressing over the squid mixture. Toss gently and leave for at least 5 minutes. Add salt to taste and serve warm or cold.

Squid with Broccoli

The slightly chewy squid contrasts beautifully with the crisp crunch of the broccoli to give this dish the perfect combination of textures so beloved by the Chinese.

Serves 4

INGREDIENTS
300 ml/¹/₂ pint/1¹/₄ cups fish stock
350 g/12 oz prepared squid, cut into
    large pieces
225 g/8 oz broccoli
15 ml/1 tbsp vegetable oil
2 garlic cloves, finely chopped
15 ml/1 tbsp dry sherry
10 ml/2 tsp cornflour
2.5 ml/¹/₂ tsp caster sugar
45 ml/3 tbsp cold water
15 ml/1 tbsp oyster sauce
2.5 ml/¹/₂ tsp sesame oil
noodles, to serve

fish stock

broccoli

squid

vegetable oil

garlic

sherry

cornflour

caster sugar

oyster sauce

sesame oil

1 Bring the fish stock to the boil in a wok or saucepan. Cook the squid pieces for 2 minutes until they are tender and have curled. Drain and set aside.

2 Trim the broccoli and cut into small florets. Cook in a saucepan of boiling water for 2 minutes until crisp-tender. Drain thoroughly.

NUTRITIONAL NOTES
PER PORTION:

ENERGY 153 Kcals/781 KJ **FAT** 6.5 g
SATURATED FAT 0.8 g
CHOLESTEROL 197 mg

3 Heat the vegetable oil in a wok or non-stick frying pan. Stir-fry the garlic for a few seconds, then add the squid, broccoli and sherry. Stir-fry for about 2 minutes.

4 Mix the cornflour and sugar to a paste with the water. Stir the mixture into the wok or pan, with the oyster sauce. Cook, stirring, until the sauce thickens slightly. Just before serving, stir in the sesame oil. Serve with noodles.

Monkfish and Scallop Skewers

Using lemon grass stalks as skewers imbues the seafood with a subtle citrus flavour.

Serves 4

INGREDIENTS
450 g/1 lb monkfish fillet
8 lemon grass stalks
30 ml/2 tbsp fresh lemon juice
15 ml/1 tbsp olive oil
15 ml/1 tbsp finely chopped
  fresh coriander
2.5 ml/¹⁄₂ tsp salt
large pinch of ground black pepper
12 large scallops, halved crossways
fresh coriander leaves, to garnish
rice, to serve

lemon grass

olive oil

monkfish

coriander

scallops

lemon

NUTRITIONAL NOTES
PER PORTION:

ENERGY 348 Kcals/1476 KJ FAT 6.1 g
SATURATED FAT 2 g
CHOLESTEROL 114 mg

1 Remove any membrane from the monkfish, then cut into 16 large chunks.

2 Remove the outer leaves from the lemon grass to leave thin rigid stalks. Chop the tender parts of the lemon grass leaves finely and place in a bowl. Stir in the lemon juice, oil, chopped coriander, salt and pepper.

VARIATION
Raw tiger prawns and salmon make an excellent alternative ingredient for the skewers, with or without the monkfish.

3 Thread the fish and scallop chunks alternately on the eight lemon grass stalks. Arrange the skewers of fish and shellfish in a shallow dish and pour over the marinade.

4 Cover and leave in a cool place for 1 hour, turning occasionally. Transfer the skewers to a heatproof dish or bamboo steamer, cover and steam over boiling water for 10 minutes until just cooked. Garnish with coriander and serve with rice and the cooking juice poured over.

Salt "Baked" Chicken

This is a wonderful way of cooking chicken. All the delicious, succulent juices are sealed inside the salt crust – yet the flavour isn't salty.

Serves 8

INGREDIENTS

1.5 kg/3–3½ lb corn-fed chicken
1.5 ml/¼ tsp fine sea salt
2.25 kg/5 lb coarse rock salt
15 ml/1 tbsp vegetable oil
2.5 cm/1 in piece fresh root ginger, finely chopped
4 spring onions, cut into fine rings
boiled rice, garnished with shredded spring onions, to serve

chicken

spring onions

root ginger

rock salt

COOK'S TIP

To reduce the fat content, remove and discard the skin from the chicken before eating.

NUTRITIONAL NOTES

PER PORTION:

ENERGY 284 Kcals/1256 KJ **FAT** 18.8 g
SATURATED FAT 5.4 g
CHOLESTEROL 128 mg

1 Rinse the chicken. Pat it dry, both inside and out, with kitchen paper, then rub the inside with the sea salt.

2 Place four pieces of damp kitchen paper on the bottom of a heavy-based frying pan or wok just large enough to hold the chicken.

3 Sprinkle a layer of rock salt over the kitchen paper, about 1 cm/½ in thick. Place the chicken on top of the salt.

4 Pour the remaining salt over the chicken until it is completely covered. Dampen six more pieces of kitchen paper and place these around the rim of the pan or wok. Cover with a tight-fitting lid. Put the pan or wok over a high heat for 10 minutes or until it gives off a slightly smoky smell.

5 Immediately reduce the heat to medium and continue to cook the chicken for 30 minutes without lifting the lid. After 30 minutes, turn off the heat and leave for a further 10 minutes before carefully lifting the chicken out of the salt. Brush off any salt still clinging to the chicken and allow the bird to cool for 20 minutes before cutting it into serving-size pieces.

6 Heat the oil in a small saucepan until very hot. Add the ginger and spring onions and fry for a few seconds, then pour into a heatproof bowl and use as a dipping sauce for the chicken. Serve the chicken with boiled rice, garnished with shredded spring onions.

COOK'S TIP

The dry salt around the top of the chicken can be used again, but the salt from under the bird should be thrown away, as this will have absorbed fat and cooking juices.

Chicken with Cashew Nuts

An all-time favourite, this classic dish is no less tasty when given the low fat treatment.

Serves 4

INGREDIENTS
350 g/12 oz skinless chicken
    breast fillets
1.5 ml/¼ tsp salt
pinch of ground white pepper
15 ml/1 tbsp dry sherry
300 ml/½ pint/1¼ cups chicken
    stock
15 ml/1 tbsp vegetable oil
1 garlic clove, finely chopped
1 small carrot, cut into cubes
½ cucumber, about 75 g/3 oz, cut
    into 1 cm/½ in cubes
50 g/2 oz/½ cup drained canned
    bamboo shoots, cut into
    1 cm/½ in cubes
5 ml/1 tsp cornflour
15 ml/1 tbsp light soy sauce
5 ml/1 tsp caster sugar
25 g/1 oz/¼ cup dry roasted
    cashew nuts
2.5 ml/½ tsp sesame oil
noodles, to serve

garlic

chicken breast fillets

chicken stock

cashew nuts

soy sauce

caster sugar

cucumber

sherry

sesame oil

cornflour   carrot

1 Cut the chicken into 2 cm/¾ in cubes. Place the cubes in a bowl, stir in the salt, pepper and sherry, cover and marinate for 15 minutes.

2 Bring the stock to the boil in a large saucepan. Add the chicken and cook, stirring, for 3 minutes. Drain, reserving 90 ml/6 tbsp of the stock, and set aside.

NUTRITIONAL NOTES

PER PORTION:

ENERGY 223 Kcals/1073 KJ **FAT** 8.5 g
SATURATED FAT 1.5 g
CHOLESTEROL 0.8 mg

3 Heat the vegetable oil in a non-stick frying pan until very hot, add the garlic and stir-fry for a few seconds. Add the carrot, cucumber and bamboo shoots and continue to stir-fry over a medium heat for 2 minutes.

4 Stir in the chicken and reserved stock. Mix the cornflour with the soy sauce and sugar and add the mixture to the pan. Cook, stirring, until the sauce thickens slightly. Finally, add the cashew nuts and sesame oil. Toss to mix thoroughly, then serve with noodles.

Chicken with Lemon Sauce

Succulent chicken with a refreshing lemony sauce and just a hint of lime is a sure winner.

Serves 4

INGREDIENTS
4 small skinless chicken breast fillets
5 ml/1 tsp sesame oil
15 ml/1 tbsp dry sherry
1 egg white, lightly beaten
30 ml/2 tbsp cornflour
15 ml/1 tbsp vegetable oil
salt and ground white pepper
chopped coriander leaves and
    spring onions and lemon wedges,
    to garnish

FOR THE SAUCE
45 ml/3 tbsp fresh lemon juice
30 ml/2 tbsp lime cordial
45 ml/3 tbsp caster sugar
10 ml/2 tsp cornflour
90 ml/6 tbsp cold water

sherry

*chicken
breast fillets*

lime cordial

lemon *egg*

sesame oil

cornflour *caster sugar*

NUTRITIONAL NOTES
PER PORTION:

ENERGY 314 Kcals/1464 KJ FAT 6.5 g
SATURATED FAT 1.2 g
CHOLESTEROL 117 mg

1 Arrange the chicken breasts in a single layer in a shallow bowl. Mix the sesame oil with the sherry and add 2.5 ml/½ tsp salt and 1.5 ml/¼ tsp pepper. Pour over the chicken, cover and marinate for 15 minutes.

2 Mix together the egg white and cornflour. Add the mixture to the chicken and turn the chicken with tongs until thoroughly coated. Heat the vegetable oil in a non-stick frying pan or wok and fry the chicken fillets for about 15 minutes until the fillets are golden brown on both sides.

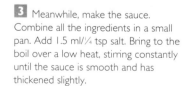

3 Meanwhile, make the sauce. Combine all the ingredients in a small pan. Add 1.5 ml/¼ tsp salt. Bring to the boil over a low heat, stirring constantly until the sauce is smooth and has thickened slightly.

4 Cut the chicken into pieces and arrange on a warm serving plate. Pour the sauce over, garnish with the coriander leaves, spring onions and lemon wedges and serve.

Chicken with Mixed Vegetables

A riot of colour, this delectable dish has plenty of contrasts in terms of texture and taste.

Serves 4

INGREDIENTS
350 g/12 oz skinless chicken
    breast fillets
20 ml/4 tsp vegetable oil
300 ml/½ pint/1¼ cups chicken stock
75 g/3 oz/¾ cup drained, canned
    straw mushrooms
50 g/2 oz/½ cup sliced, drained,
    canned bamboo shoots
50 g/2 oz/⅓ cup drained, canned
    water chestnuts, sliced
1 small carrot, sliced
50 g/2 oz/½ cup mangetouts
15 ml/1 tbsp dry sherry
15 ml/1 tbsp oyster sauce
5 ml/1 tsp caster sugar
5 ml/1 tsp cornflour
15 ml/1 tbsp cold water
salt and ground white pepper

chicken stock

straw mushrooms

chicken breast fillets

bamboo shoots

water chestnuts

mangetouts *cornflour*

caster sugar *oyster sauce* *sherry* *carrot*

1 Put the chicken in a shallow bowl. Add 5 ml/1 tsp of the oil, 1.5 ml/¼ tsp salt and a pinch of pepper. Cover and set aside for 10 minutes in a cool place.

2 Bring the stock to the boil in a saucepan. Add the chicken and cook for 12 minutes, or until tender. Drain and slice, reserving 75 ml/5 tbsp of the stock.

NUTRITIONAL NOTES
PER PORTION:

ENERGY 198 Kcals/836 KJ **FAT** 6 g
SATURATED FAT 1.8 g
CHOLESTEROL 52 mg

3 Heat the remaining oil in a non-stick frying pan or wok, add all the vegetables and stir-fry for 2 minutes. Stir in the sherry, oyster sauce, caster sugar and reserved stock. Add the chicken to the pan and cook for 2 minutes more.

4 Mix the cornflour to a paste with the water. Add the mixture to the pan and cook, stirring, until the sauce thickens slightly. Season to taste with salt and pepper and serve immediately.

Duck with Pineapple

Duck and pineapple is a favourite combination, but the fruit must not be allowed to dominate. Here the proportions are perfect and the dish has a wonderfully subtle sweet-sour flavour.

Serves 4

INGREDIENTS
15 ml/1 tbsp dry sherry
15 ml/1 tbsp dark soy sauce
2 small skinless duck breasts
15 ml/1 tbsp vegetable oil
2 garlic cloves, finely chopped
1 small onion, sliced
1 red pepper, seeded and cut into
    2.5 cm/1 in squares
75 g/3 oz/½ cup drained, canned
    pineapple chunks
90 ml/6 tbsp pineapple juice
15 ml/1 tbsp rice vinegar
5 ml/1 tsp cornflour
15 ml/1 tbsp cold water
5 ml/1 tsp sesame oil
salt and ground white pepper
1 spring onion, shredded, to garnish

red pepper
duck breasts
onion
garlic
sherry
rice vinegar
soy sauce
pineapple juice
cornflour
pineapple chunks
sesame oil

NUTRITIONAL NOTES
PER PORTION:

ENERGY 166 Kcals/832 KJ **FAT** 8 g
SATURATED FAT 1.7 g
CHOLESTEROL 71 mg

1 Mix together the sherry and soy sauce. Stir in 2.5 ml/½ tsp salt and 1.5 ml/¼ tsp pepper. Put the duck breasts in a bowl and add the marinade. Cover and leave in a cool place for 1 hour.

2 Drain the duck breasts and place them on a rack in a grill pan. Grill under a medium to high heat for 10 minutes on each side. Allow to cool for 10 minutes, then cut into bite-size pieces.

3 Heat the vegetable oil in a non-stick frying pan or wok and stir-fry the garlic and onion for 1 minute. Add the red pepper, pineapple chunks, duck, pineapple juice and vinegar and stir-fry for 2 minutes.

4 Mix the cornflour to a paste with the water. Add the mixture to the pan with 1.5 ml/¼ tsp salt. Cook, stirring, until the sauce thickens. Stir in the sesame oil and serve at once, garnished with spring onion shreds.

Duck with Pancakes

Considerably lower in fat than traditional Peking Duck, but just as delicious. Guests spread their pancakes with sauce, add duck and vegetables, then roll them up.

NUTRITIONAL NOTES

PER PORTION:

ENERGY 169 Kcals/757 KJ **FAT** 13.5 g
SATURATED FAT 1.6 g
CHOLESTEROL 71 mg

Serves 4

INGREDIENTS
15 ml/1 tbsp clear honey
1.5 ml/1¼ tsp five spice powder
1 garlic clove, finely chopped
15 ml/1 tbsp hoisin sauce
2.5 ml/½ tsp salt
a large pinch of ground
    white pepper
2 small skinless duck breasts
½ cucumber
10 spring onions
3 Chinese leaves
12 Chinese pancakes (see
    Cook's Tip)

FOR THE SAUCE
5 ml/1 tsp vegetable oil
2 garlic cloves, chopped
2 spring onions, chopped
1 cm/½ in piece of fresh root
    ginger, bruised
60 ml/4 tbsp hoisin sauce
15 ml/1 tbsp dry sherry
15 ml/1 tbsp cold water
2.5 ml/½ tsp sesame oil

sesame oil

hoisin sauce

duck breasts

root ginger

sherry

five spice powder

Chinese leaves

spring onions

honey

garlic

cucumber

Chinese pancakes

1 Mix the honey, five spice powder, garlic, hoisin sauce, salt and pepper in a shallow dish large enough to hold the duck breasts side by side. Add the duck breasts, turning them in the marinade. Cover and leave in a cool place to marinate for 2 hours.

2 Cut the cucumber in half lengthways. Using a teaspoon scrape out and discard the seeds. Cut the flesh into thin batons 5 cm/2 in long.

3 Cut off and discard the green tops from the spring onions. Finely shred the white parts and place on a serving plate with the cucumber batons.

4 Make the sauce. Heat the oil in a small saucepan and gently fry the garlic for a few seconds without browning. Add the spring onions, ginger, hoisin sauce, sherry and water. Cook gently for 5 minutes, stirring often, then strain and mix with the sesame oil.

5 Remove the duck breasts from the marinade and drain them well. Place the duck breasts on a rack over a grill pan. Grill under a medium to high heat for 8–10 minutes on each side. Allow to cool for 5 minutes before cutting into thin slices. Arrange on a serving platter, cover and keep warm.

COOK'S TIP
Chinese pancakes can be bought frozen from Chinese supermarkets. Leave to thaw before steaming.

6 Line a steamer with the Chinese leaves and place the pancakes on top. Have ready a large pan with 5 cm/2 in boiling water. Cover the steamer and place on a trivet in the pan. Steam over a high heat for 2 minutes or until the pancakes are hot. Serve at once with the duck, cucumber, spring onions and sauce.

Char-siu Pork

Marinated pork, roasted and glazed with honey, is irresistible on its own and can also be used as the basis for salads or stir-fries.

Serves 6

INGREDIENTS
15 ml/1 tbsp vegetable oil
15 ml/1 tbsp hoisin sauce
15 ml/1 tbsp yellow bean sauce
1.5 ml/¼ tsp five spice powder
2.5 ml/½ tsp cornflour
15 ml/1 tbsp caster sugar
1.5 ml/¼ tsp salt
1.5 ml/¼ tsp ground white pepper
450 g/1 lb pork fillet, trimmed
10 ml/2 tsp clear honey
shredded spring onion, to garnish
rice, to serve

pork fillet

vegetable oil

hoisin sauce

yellow bean sauce

five spice powder

caster sugar

cornflour

honey

NUTRITIONAL NOTES
PER PORTION:

ENERGY 145 Kcals/702 KJ **FAT** 6.8 g
SATURATED FAT 1.9 g
CHOLESTEROL 53 mg

1 Mix the oil, sauces, five spice powder, cornflour, sugar and seasoning in a shallow dish. Add the pork and coat it with the mixture. Cover and chill for 4 hours or overnight.

2 Preheat the oven to 190°C/375°F/ Gas 5. Drain the pork and place it on a wire rack over a deep roasting tin. Roast for 40 minutes, turning the pork over from time to time.

3 Check that the pork is cooked by inserting a skewer or fork into the meat; the juices should run clear. If they are still tinged with pink, roast the pork for 5–10 minutes more.

4 Remove the pork from the oven and brush it with the honey. Allow to cool for 10 minutes before cutting into thin slices. Garnish with spring onion and serve hot or cold with rice.

Sticky Pork Ribs

A delicious dish which has to be eaten with the fingers to be enjoyed fully.

Serves 4

INGREDIENTS
30 ml/2 tbsp caster sugar
2.5 ml/½ tsp five spice powder
45 ml/3 tbsp hoisin sauce
30 ml/2 tbsp yellow bean sauce
3 garlic cloves, finely chopped
15 ml/1 tbsp cornflour
2.5 ml/½ tsp salt
16 pork ribs
chives and sliced spring onion,
    to garnish
salad or rice, to serve

pork ribs

hoisin sauce

five spice powder

yellow bean sauce

caster sugar

cornflour

garlic

NUTRITIONAL NOTES
PER PORTION:

ENERGY 239 Kcals/1004 KJ **FAT** 6.3 g
SATURATED FAT 1.6 g
CHOLESTEROL 43.0 mg

1 Combine the caster sugar, five spice powder, hoisin sauce, yellow bean sauce, garlic, cornflour and salt in a bowl, then mix together well.

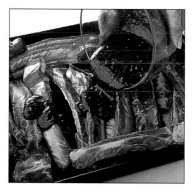

2 Place the pork ribs in an ovenproof dish and pour the marinade over. Mix thoroughly, cover and leave in a cool place for 1 hour.

COOK'S TIP
The ribs barbecue well. Bake as described in Step 3, then transfer them to the barbecue to finish cooking. The sauce coating makes the ribs liable to burn, so watch them closely.

3 Preheat the oven to 180°C/350°F/Gas 4. Cover the dish tightly with foil and bake the pork ribs for 40 minutes. Baste the ribs from time to time with the cooking juices.

4 Remove the foil, baste the ribs and continue to cook for 20 minutes until glossy and brown. Garnish with chives and spring onion and serve with a salad or rice.

Sweet-and-Sour Pork

A wonderful low fat version of this popular, classic Chinese dish.

Serves 4

INGREDIENTS
15 ml/1 tbsp dry sherry
350 g/12 oz lean pork steaks
15 ml/1 tbsp vegetable oil
1 garlic clove, finely chopped
½ onion, diced
1 small green pepper, seeded and
    cut into 2.5 cm/1 in squares
1 small carrot, sliced
75 g/3 oz/½ cup drained, canned
    pineapple chunks
30 ml/2 tbsp malt vinegar
45 ml/3 tbsp tomato ketchup
150 ml/¼ pint/⅔ cup pineapple
    juice
10 ml/2 tsp caster sugar
10 ml/2 tsp cornflour
15 ml/1 tbsp cold water
salt and ground black pepper
rice, to serve

garlic
pork steaks
sherry
onion
caster sugar
carrot
pineapple juice
cornflour
malt vinegar
green pepper
pineapple chunks
ketchup

1 Mix the sherry, 2.5 ml/½ tsp salt and a large pinch of pepper in a shallow dish. Add the pork, turn to coat, then cover and leave to marinate in a cool place for 15 minutes.

2 Drain the pork steaks and place them on a rack over a grill pan. Grill under a high heat for 5 minutes on each side or until cooked, then remove and leave to cool. Cut the cooked pork into bite-size pieces.

4 Stir in the pineapple chunks, vinegar, ketchup, pineapple juice and caster sugar. Bring to the boil, lower the heat and simmer for 3 minutes.

5 Add the cooked pork to the vegetable mixture and cook for about 2 minutes.

COOK'S TIP
This is a great way of giving leftover pork from the Sunday roast a new lease of life. Proceed from step 3.

3 Heat the oil in a non-stick frying pan or wok until very hot. Stir-fry the garlic and onion for a few seconds, then add the green pepper and carrot and stir-fry for 1 minute.

6 Mix the cornflour to a paste with the water. Add the mixture to the pan or wok and cook, stirring, until slightly thickened. Serve with rice.

NUTRITIONAL NOTES
PER PORTION:
ENERGY 258 Kcals/1225 KJ **FAT** 8.5 g
SATURATED FAT 2.2 g
CHOLESTEROL 66 mg

Savoury Chiffon Custards

The velvety smoothness of the egg combined with the coarse texture of the minced pork makes this a children's favourite.

Serves 4

INGREDIENTS
4 dried Chinese mushrooms
175 g/6 oz lean pork,
   roughly chopped
15 g/½ oz dried shrimps, soaked
   in warm water
3 large eggs
475 ml/16 fl oz/2 cups chicken stock
salt and ground white pepper
30ml/2 tbsp snipped chives
plaited whole chives, to garnish

dried shrimps

eggs

pork

chicken stock

dried Chinese mushrooms

chives

NUTRITIONAL NOTES
PER PORTION:

ENERGY 183 Kcals/769 KJ FAT 7.2 g
SATURATED FAT 2 g
CHOLESTEROL 234 mg

1 Soak the mushrooms in a bowl of hot water for 30 minutes until soft. Drain, remove the hard stems, then cut the mushroom caps into small pieces.

2 Place the pork and mushrooms in a food processor. Drain the shrimps and add them to the processor with 1.5 ml/¼ tsp salt and a pinch of pepper. Process until finely ground. Scrape into a bowl and set aside.

3 Break the eggs into a mixing bowl, then gradually whisk in the stock. Add 2.5 ml/½ tsp salt and a large pinch of pepper. Beat well, then strain through a fine sieve into a jug.

4 Stir a little of the beaten egg mixture into the pork mixture to loosen it. Divide the pork among four 300 ml/½ pint/1¼ cup soufflé dishes and pour the remaining egg mixture over, dividing it equally among the soufflé dishes.

5 Sprinkle the snipped chives over the top. Cover the dishes tightly with clear film and then foil and place in a steamer.

6 Have ready a pan with about 5 cm/2 in boiling water. Cover the steamer and steam over boiling water for about 10 minutes, then lower the heat and continue steaming steadily for a further 20 minutes until the custards are just set. Serve immediately, garnished with plaited whole chives.

VARIATION
For a delicious alternative, replace the pork mixture with fresh or frozen white crabmeat; this gives a more subtle taste. The crabmeat custards would make a great starter.

Beef with Peppers and Black Bean Sauce

A spicy, rich dish with the distinctive flavour of black bean sauce.

Serves 4

INGREDIENTS

350 g/12 oz rump steak, trimmed
    and thinly sliced
15 ml/1 tbsp vegetable oil
300 ml/½ pint/1¼ cups beef stock
2 garlic cloves, finely chopped
5 ml/1 tsp grated fresh root ginger
1 fresh red chilli, seeded
    and finely chopped
15 ml/1 tbsp black bean sauce
1 green pepper, seeded and cut into
    2.5 cm/1 in squares
15 ml/1 tbsp dry sherry
5 ml/1 tsp cornflour
5 ml/1 tsp caster sugar
45 ml/3 tbsp cold water
salt
rice noodles, to serve

beef stock

rump steak

ginger

garlic

black bean sauce

sherry

cornflour

pepper

chilli

caster sugar

NUTRITIONAL NOTES
PER PORTION:

ENERGY 161 Kcals/818 KJ FAT 6.7 g
SATURATED FAT 1.8 g
CHOLESTEROL 52 mg

1 Place the steak in a bowl. Add 5 ml/1 tsp of the oil and stir to coat.

2 Bring the stock to the boil in a saucepan. Add the beef and cook for 2 minutes, stirring constantly to prevent the slices from sticking together. Drain the beef and set aside.

COOK'S TIP

For extra colour, use half each of a green pepper and red pepper or a mixture that includes yellow and orange

3 Heat the remaining oil in a non-stick frying pan or wok. Stir-fry the garlic, ginger and chilli with the black bean sauce for a few seconds. Add the pepper squares and a little water. Cook for about 2 minutes more, then stir in the sherry. Add the beef slices to the pan and spoon the sauce over.

4 Mix the cornflour and sugar to a paste with the water. Pour the mixture into the pan. Cook, stirring, until the sauce has thickened. Season with salt. Serve at once, with rice noodles.

Beef with Tomatoes

Colourful and fresh-tasting, this is the perfect way of serving sun-ripened tomatoes from the garden.

Serves 4

INGREDIENTS
350 g/12 oz rump steak, trimmed
15 ml/1 tbsp vegetable oil
300 ml/½ pint/1¼ cups beef stock
1 garlic clove, finely chopped
1 small onion, sliced into rings
5 tomatoes, quartered
15 ml/1 tbsp tomato purée
5 ml/1 tsp caster sugar
15 ml/1 tbsp dry sherry
15 ml/1 tbsp cold water
salt and ground white pepper
noodles, to serve

beef stock

onion

garlic

tomatoes

rump steak

tomato purée

caster sugar

sherry

NUTRITIONAL NOTES
PER PORTION:

ENERGY 171 Kcals/870 KJ **FAT** 6.8 g
SATURATED FAT 1.8 g
CHOLESTEROL 52 mg

1 Slice the rump steak thinly. Place the slices in a bowl, add 5 ml/1 tsp of the vegetable oil and stir to coat.

2 Bring the stock to the boil in a saucepan. Add the beef and cook for 2 minutes, stirring constantly. Drain the beef and set it aside.

COOK'S TIP
Use plum tomatoes or vine tomatoes from the garden, if you can. The store-bought ones are a little more expensive than standard tomatoes but have a far better flavour.

3 Heat the remaining oil in a non-stick frying pan or wok until very hot. Stir-fry the garlic and onion for a few seconds.

4 Add the beef and tomatoes and cook for 1 minute more. Mix the tomato purée, sugar, sherry and water in a cup or small bowl. Stir the mixture into the pan, add salt and pepper to taste and mix thoroughly. Cook for 1 minute, then serve with noodles.

Beef in Oyster Sauce

The oyster sauce gives the beef extra richness and depth of flavour. To complete the dish, all you need is plain boiled rice or noodles.

Serves 4

INGREDIENTS

350 g/12 oz rump steak, trimmed
15 ml/1 tbsp vegetable oil
300 ml/½ pint/1¼ cups beef stock
2 garlic cloves, finely chopped
1 small carrot, thinly sliced
3 celery sticks, sliced
15 ml/1 tbsp dry sherry
5 ml/1 tsp caster sugar
45 ml/3 tbsp oyster sauce
5 ml/1 tsp cornflour
15 ml/1 tbsp cold water
4 spring onions, cut into
    2.5 cm/1 in lengths
ground white pepper
rice or noodles, to serve

rump steak

celery *carrot* *vegetable oil*

caster sugar *oyster sauce* *garlic*

spring onions

cornflour *beef stock* *sherry*

VARIATION
To increase the number of servings without upping the fat content of the dish, add more vegetables, such as peppers, mangetouts, water chestnuts, baby corn cobs and mushrooms.

1 Slice the steak thinly. Place the slices in a bowl, add 5 ml/1 tsp of the vegetable oil and stir to coat.

2 Bring the stock to the boil in a large saucepan. Add the beef and cook, stirring, for 2 minutes. Drain, reserving 45 ml/3 tbsp of the stock, and set aside.

3 Heat the remaining oil in a non-stick frying pan or wok. Stir-fry the garlic for a few seconds, then add the carrot and celery and stir-fry for 2 minutes.

4 Stir in the sherry, caster sugar, oyster sauce and a large pinch of pepper. Add the steak to the pan with the reserved stock. Simmer for 2 minutes.

5 Mix the cornflour to a paste with the water. Add the mixture to the pan and cook, stirring, until thickened.

6 Stir in the spring onions, mixing well, then serve at once, with rice or noodles.

NUTRITIONAL NOTES
PER PORTION:

ENERGY 167 Kcals/836 KJ **FAT** 6.6 g
SATURATED FAT 0.5 g
CHOLESTEROL 5.2 mg

Broccoli with Soy Sauce

A wonderfully simple dish that you will want to make again and again. The broccoli cooks in next-to-no-time, so don't start cooking until you are almost ready to eat.

Serves 4

INGREDIENTS
450 g/1 lb broccoli
15 ml/1 tbsp vegetable oil
2 garlic cloves, crushed
30 ml/2 tbsp light soy sauce
salt
fried garlic slices, to garnish

broccoli

garlic

vegetable oil

soy sauce

NUTRITIONAL NOTES
Per portion:

ENERGY 68 Kcals/420 KJ **FAT** 3.8 g
SATURATED FAT 0.5 g
CHOLESTEROL 0 mg

1 Trim the thick stems of the broccoli; cut the head into large florets.

2 Bring a saucepan of lightly salted water to the boil. Add the broccoli and cook for 3–4 minutes until crisp-tender.

VARIATION
Most leafy vegetables taste delicious prepared this way. Try blanched cos lettuce and you may be surprised at how crisp and clean the taste is.

3 Drain the broccoli thoroughly and arrange in a heated serving dish.

4 Heat the oil in a small saucepan. Fry the garlic for 2 minutes to release the flavour, then remove it with a slotted spoon. Pour the oil carefully over the broccoli, taking care as it will splatter. Drizzle the soy sauce over the broccoli, scatter over the fried garlic and serve.

Stir-fried Beansprouts

This fresh, crunchy vegetable, which is almost synonymous with Chinese restaurants, tastes much better when stir-fried at home.

Serves 4

INGREDIENTS

15 ml/1 tbsp vegetable oil
1 garlic clove, finely chopped
5 ml/1 tsp grated fresh root ginger
1 small carrot, cut into fine matchsticks
50 g/2 oz/½ cup drained, canned bamboo shoots, cut into fine matchsticks
450 g/1 lb/8 cups beansprouts
2.5 ml/½ tsp salt
large pinch of ground white pepper
15 ml/1 tbsp dry sherry
15 ml/1 tbsp light soy sauce
2.5 ml/½ tsp sesame oil

bamboo shoots

beansprouts

carrot

sesame oil

root ginger

garlic

soy sauce

sherry

NUTRITIONAL NOTES
PER PORTION:

ENERGY 54 Kcals/362 KJ **FAT** 3.5 g
SATURATED FAT 0.5 g
CHOLESTEROL 0 mg

1 Heat the vegetable oil in a non-stick frying pan or wok. Add the chopped garlic and grated ginger and stir-fry for a few minutes.

2 Add the carrot and bamboo shoot matchsticks to the pan or wok and stir-fry for a few minutes.

COOK'S TIP
Beansprouts keep best when stored in the fridge or other cool place in a bowl of cold water, but you must remember to change the water daily.

3 Add the beansprouts to the pan or wok with the salt and pepper. Drizzle over the sherry and toss the beansprouts over the heat for 3 minutes until hot.

4 Sprinkle over the soy sauce and sesame oil, toss to mix thoroughly, then serve at once.

Braised Bean Curd with Mushrooms

The mushrooms flavour the bean curd beautifully to make this the perfect vegetarian main course.

Serves 4

INGREDIENTS

350 g/12 oz bean curd (tofu)
2.5 ml/½ tsp sesame oil
10 ml/2 tsp light soy sauce
15 ml/1 tbsp vegetable oil
2 garlic cloves, finely chopped
2.5 ml/½ tsp grated fresh root ginger
115 g/4 oz/1 cup fresh shiitake
    mushrooms, stalks removed
175 g/6 oz/1½ cups fresh oyster
    mushrooms
115 g/4 oz/1 cup drained, canned
    straw mushrooms
115 g/4 oz/1 cup button
    mushrooms, cut in half
15 ml/1 tbsp dry sherry
15 ml/1 tbsp dark soy sauce
90 ml/6 tbsp vegetable stock
5 ml/1 tsp cornflour
15 ml/1 tbsp cold water
salt and ground white pepper
2 spring onions, shredded

1 Put the bean curd in a dish and sprinkle with the sesame oil, light soy sauce and a large pinch of pepper. Leave to marinate for 10 minutes, then drain and cut into 2.5 x 1 cm/1 x ½ in pieces.

2 Heat the vegetable oil in a non-stick frying pan or wok. When it is very hot, fry the garlic and ginger for a few seconds. Add all the mushrooms and stir-fry for 2 minutes.

3 Stir in the sherry, soy sauce and stock, with salt, if needed, and pepper. Simmer for 4 minutes.

4 Mix the cornflour to a paste with the water. Stir the mixture into the pan or wok and cook, stirring, until thickened.

shiitake mushrooms

button mushrooms

oyster mushrooms

straw mushrooms

bean curd

vegetable stock

garlic

cornflour   *dark soy sauce*   *sesame oil*

light soy sauce

root ginger

spring onions

sherry

NUTRITIONAL NOTES

PER PORTION:

ENERGY 207 Kcals/1001 KJ **FAT** 7.7 g
SATURATED FAT 0.8 g
CHOLESTEROL 0 mg

COOK'S TIP

If fresh shiitake mushrooms are not available, use dried Chinese mushrooms soaked in hot water. Use the soaking liquid instead of vegetable stock for a more intense flavour.

5 Carefully add the pieces of bean curd, toss gently to coat thoroughly and simmer for 2 minutes.

6 Scatter the shredded spring onions over the top of the mixture, transfer to a serving dish and serve immediately.

Stir-fried Chinese Leaves

This simple way of cooking Chinese leaves preserves their delicate flavour.

Serves 4

INGREDIENTS
675 g/1½ lb Chinese leaves
15 ml/1 tbsp vegetable oil
2 garlic cloves, finely chopped
2.5 cm/1 in piece of fresh root
 ginger, finely chopped
2.5 ml/½ tsp salt
15 ml/1 tbsp oyster sauce
4 spring onions, cut into
 2.5 cm/1 in lengths

*Chinese
leaves*

garlic

root ginger

oyster sauce

spring onions

1 Stack the Chinese leaves together and cut them into 2.5 cm/1 in slices.

2 Heat the oil in a wok or large deep saucepan. Stir-fry the garlic and ginger for 1 minute.

NUTRITIONAL NOTES
PER PORTION:

ENERGY 53 Kcals/358 KJ FAT 3.1 g
SATURATED FAT 0.3 g
CHOLESTEROL 0 mg

COOK'S TIP
For guests who are vegetarian, substitute 15 ml/1 tbsp light soy sauce and 5 ml/1 tsp of caster sugar for the oyster sauce.

3 Add the Chinese leaves to the wok or saucepan and stir-fry for 2 minutes. Sprinkle the salt over and drizzle with the oyster sauce. Toss the leaves over the heat for 2 minutes more.

4 Stir in the spring onions. Toss the mixture well, transfer it to a heated serving plate and serve.

Sautéed Green Beans

The smoky flavour of the dried shrimps adds an extra dimension to green beans cooked this way.

Serves 4

INGREDIENTS
450 g/1 lb green beans
15 ml/1 tbsp vegetable oil
3 garlic cloves, finely chopped
5 spring onions, cut into
    2.5 cm/1 in lengths
25 g/1 oz dried shrimps, soaked in
    warm water and drained
15 ml/1 tbsp light soy sauce
salt

green beans

soy sauce

garlic

spring onions

dried shrimps

1 Trim the green beans. Cut each green bean in half.

2 Bring a saucepan of lightly salted water to the boil and cook the beans for 3–4 minutes until crisp-tender. Drain, refresh under cold water and drain again.

3 Heat the oil in a non-stick frying pan or wok until very hot. Stir-fry the garlic and spring onions for 30 seconds, then add the shrimps. Mix lightly.

4 Add the green beans and soy sauce. Toss the mixture over the heat until the beans are hot. Serve at once.

NUTRITIONAL NOTES
PER PORTION:

ENERGY 76 Kcals/453 KJ **FAT** 3.5 g
SATURATED FAT 0.4 g
CHOLESTEROL 31.5 mg

COOK'S TIP
Don't be tempted to use too many dried shrimps. Their flavour is very strong and could overwhelm the more delicate taste of the beans.

Braised Aubergine and Courgettes

Aubergine, courgettes and some fresh red chillies form the basis of a dish that is simple, spicy and quite sensational.

Serves 4

INGREDIENTS
1 aubergine, about 350 g/12 oz
2 small courgettes
15 ml/1 tbsp vegetable oil
2 garlic cloves, finely chopped
2 fresh red chillies, seeded
    and finely chopped
1 small onion, diced
15 ml/1 tbsp black bean sauce
15 ml/1 tbsp dark soy sauce
45 ml/3 tbsp cold water
salt
chilli flowers (optional), to garnish
    (see Cook's Tip)

aubergine

courgettes

onion

chillies

vegetable oil

garlic

black bean sauce

soy sauce

1 Trim the aubergine and slice it in half lengthways, then across into 1 cm/½ in thick slices. Layer the slices in a colander, sprinkling each layer with salt. Leave the aubergine in the sink to stand for about 20 minutes.

2 Roll cut the courgettes by slicing off the one end diagonally, then rolling the courgette through 180° and taking off another diagonal slice, which will form a triangular wedge. Make more wedges of courgette in the same way.

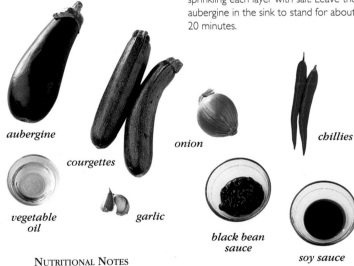

3 Rinse the aubergine slices well, drain and dry thoroughly on kitchen paper.

4 Heat the oil in a wok or non-stick frying pan. Stir-fry the garlic, chillies and onion, with the black bean sauce for a few seconds.

NUTRITIONAL NOTES
PER PORTION:

ENERGY 63 Kcals/398 KJ **FAT** 3.5 g
SATURATED FAT 0.4 g
CHOLESTEROL 0 mg

COOK'S TIP

Chilli flowers make a pretty garnish. Using a small pair of scissors, slit a fresh red chilli from the tip to within 1 cm/½ in of the stem end. Repeat this at regular intervals around the chilli so that you have slender "petals" attached at the stem. Rinse the chilli to remove the seeds, then place it in a bowl of iced water for at least 4 hours until the "petals" curl.

5 Add the aubergine slices and stir-fry for 2 minutes, sprinkling over a little water to prevent them from burning.

6 Stir in the courgettes, soy sauce and measured water. Cook, stirring occasionally, for 5 minutes. Serve hot, garnished with chilli flowers.

Mixed Vegetables Monk-style

Chinese monks eat neither meat nor fish, so "Monk-style" dishes are fine for vegetarians.

Serves 4

INGREDIENTS
50 g/2 oz dried bean curd sticks
115 g/4 oz fresh lotus root, or
   50 g/2 oz dried
10 g/¼ oz dried wood ears
8 dried Chinese mushrooms
15 ml/1 tbsp vegetable oil
75 g/3 oz/⅔ cup drained, canned
   straw mushrooms
115 g/4 oz/1 cup baby corn cobs,
   cut in half
30 ml/2 tbsp light soy sauce
15 ml/1 tbsp dry sherry
10 ml/2 tsp caster sugar
150 ml/¼ pint/⅔ cup vegetable stock
75 g/3 oz mangetouts, trimmed and
   cut in half
5 ml/1 tsp cornflour
15 ml/1 tbsp cold water
salt

1 Put the bean curd sticks in a bowl. Cover with hot water and leave to soak for 1 hour. If using fresh lotus root, peel it and slice it; if using dried lotus root, place it in a bowl of hot water and leave to soak for 1 hour.

2 Prepare the wood ears and dried Chinese mushrooms by soaking them in separate bowls of hot water for 15 minutes. Drain the wood ears, trim off and discard the hard base from each and cut the rest into bite-size pieces. Drain the soaked mushrooms, trim off and discard the stems and chop the caps roughly.

wood ears
dried bean curd sticks
soy sauce
straw mushrooms
dried Chinese mushrooms
mangetouts
cornflour
lotus root
vegetable stock
caster sugar
sherry
baby corn cobs

NUTRITIONAL NOTES
PER PORTION:

ENERGY 143 Kcals/735 KJ **FAT** 4.2 g
SATURATED FAT 0.35 g
CHOLESTEROL 0 mg

3 Drain the bean curd sticks. Cut them into 5 cm/2 in long pieces, discarding any hard pieces. If using dried lotus root, drain well.

4 Heat the oil in a non-stick frying pan or wok. Stir-fry the wood ears, Chinese mushrooms and lotus root for about 30 seconds.

COOK'S TIP
The flavour of this tasty vegetable mix improves on keeping, so any leftovers would taste even better next day.

5 Add the pieces of bean curd sticks, straw mushrooms, baby corn cobs, soy sauce, sherry, caster sugar and stock. Bring to the boil, then cover the pan or wok, lower the heat and simmer for about 20 minutes.

6 Stir in the mangetouts, with salt to taste and cook, uncovered, for 2 minutes more. Mix the cornflour to a paste with the water. Add the mixture to the pan or wok. Cook, stirring, until the sauce thickens. Serve at once.

Fried Rice with Mushrooms

A tasty rice dish that is almost a meal in itself. Sesame oil adds a hint of nutty flavour.

Serves 4

INGREDIENTS
225 g/8 oz/1¼ cups long grain rice
15 ml/1 tbsp vegetable oil
1 egg, lightly beaten
2 garlic cloves, crushed
175 g/6 oz/1¼ cups button
    mushrooms, sliced
15 ml/1 tbsp light soy sauce
1.5 ml/¼ tsp salt
2.5 ml/½ tsp sesame oil
cucumber matchsticks, to garnish

egg

garlic

long grain rice

soy sauce

sesame oil

button mushrooms

NUTRITIONAL NOTES
PER PORTION:

ENERGY 263 Kcals/1253 KJ **FAT** 5.6 g
SATURATED FAT 0.9 g
CHOLESTEROL 58.7 mg

1 Rinse the rice until the water runs clear, then drain thoroughly. Place it in a saucepan. Measure the depth of the rice against your index finger, then bring the finger up to just above the surface of the rice and add cold water to the same depth as the rice.

2 Bring the water to the boil. Stir, boil for a few minutes, then cover the pan. Lower the heat to a simmer and cook the rice gently for 5–8 minutes until all the water has been absorbed. Remove the pan from the heat and, without lifting the lid, leave for another 10 minutes before stirring or forking up the rice.

3 Heat 5 ml/1 tsp of the vegetable oil in a non-stick frying pan or wok. Add the egg and cook, stirring with a chopstick or wooden spoon until scrambled. Remove and set aside.

4 Heat the remaining vegetable oil in the pan or wok. Stir-fry the garlic for a few seconds, then add the mushrooms and stir-fry for 2 minutes, adding a little water, if needed, to prevent burning.

5 Stir in the cooked rice and cook for about 4 minutes, or until the rice is hot, stirring from time to time.

COOK'S TIP

When you cook rice this way, you may find there is a crust at the bottom of the pan. Don't worry; simply soak the crust in water for a couple of minutes to break it up, then drain it and fry it with the rest of the rice.

6 Add the scrambled egg, soy sauce, salt and sesame oil. Cook for I minute to heat through. Serve at once, garnished with cucumber matchsticks.

Sticky Rice Parcels

This is a superb dish, packed with flavour. The parcels look pretty and are a pleasure to eat.

Serves 4

INGREDIENTS

450 g/1 lb/2⅔ cups glutinous rice
20 ml/4 tsp vegetable oil
15 ml/1 tbsp dark soy sauce
1.5 ml/¼ tsp five spice powder
15 ml/1 tbsp dry sherry
4 skinless and boneless chicken thighs, each cut into 4 pieces
8 dried Chinese mushrooms, soaked in hot water until soft
25 g/1 oz dried shrimps, soaked in hot water until soft
50 g/2 oz/½ cup sliced, drained, canned bamboo shoots
300 ml/½ pint/1¼ cups chicken stock
10 ml/2 tsp cornflour
15 ml/1 tbsp cold water
4 lotus leaves, soaked in warm water until soft
salt and ground white pepper

1 Rinse the glutinous rice until the water runs clear, then leave to soak in water for 2 hours. Drain and stir in 5 ml/1 tsp of the oil and 2.5 ml/½ tsp salt. Line a large steamer with a piece of clean muslin. Transfer the rice into this. Cover and steam over boiling water for 45 minutes, stirring the rice from time to time and topping up the water if needed.

2 Mix the soy sauce, five spice powder and sherry. Put the chicken pieces in a bowl, add the marinade, stir to coat, then cover and leave to marinate for 20 minutes.

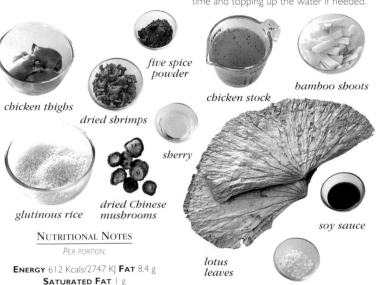

chicken thighs

dried shrimps

five spice powder

chicken stock

bamboo shoots

sherry

glutinous rice

dried Chinese mushrooms

lotus leaves

soy sauce

cornflour

NUTRITIONAL NOTES
Per portion:

ENERGY 612 Kcals/2747 KJ **FAT** 8.4 g
SATURATED FAT 1 g
CHOLESTEROL 110 mg

3 Drain the Chinese mushrooms, cut out and discard the stems, then chop the caps roughly. Drain the dried shrimps. Heat the remaining oil in a non-stick frying pan or wok. Stir-fry the chicken for 2 minutes, then add the mushrooms, shrimps, bamboo shoots and stock. Simmer for 10 minutes.

4 Mix the cornflour to a paste with the cold water. Add the mixture to the pan and cook, stirring, until the sauce has thickened. Add salt and white pepper to taste. Lift the cooked rice out of the steamer and let it cool slightly.

COOK'S TIP

The sticky rice parcels can be made several days in advance and simply re-steamed before serving. If you do this, allow an extra 20 minutes' cooking time to ensure that the filling is hot.

5 With lightly dampened hands, divide the rice into four equal portions. Put half of one portion in the centre of a lotus leaf. Spread it into a round and place a quarter of the chicken mixture on top. Cover with the remaining half portion of rice. Fold the leaf around the filling to make a neat rectangular parcel. Make three more parcels in the same way.

6 Prepare a steamer. Put the rice parcels, seam side down, into the steamer. Cover and steam over a high heat for about 30 minutes. Serve the parcels on individual heated plates, inviting each diner to unwrap their own.

Chinese Leaves and Black Rice Stir-fry

The slightly nutty, chewy black glutinous rice contrasts beautifully with the Chinese leaves.

Serves 4

INGREDIENTS

225 g/8 oz/1⅓ cups black glutinous rice or brown rice
900 ml/1½ pints/3¾ cups vegetable stock
15 ml/1 tbsp vegetable oil
225 g/8 oz Chinese leaves, cut into 1 cm/½ in strips
4 spring onions, thinly sliced
salt and ground white pepper
2.5 ml/½ tsp sesame oil

black rice

vegetable oil

sesame oil

Chinese leaves

spring onions

vegetable stock

NUTRITIONAL NOTES
PER PORTION:

ENERGY 248 Kcals/1189 KJ **FAT** 5.5 g
SATURATED FAT 0.75 g
CHOLESTEROL 0 mg

1 Rinse the rice until the water runs clear, then drain and tip into a saucepan. Add the stock and bring to the boil. Lower the heat, cover the pan and cook gently for 30 minutes. Remove from the heat and leave to stand for 15 minutes without lifting the pan lid.

2 Heat the vegetable oil in a non-stick frying pan or wok. Stir-fry the Chinese leaves for 2 minutes, adding a little water to prevent them from burning.

3 Drain the rice, stir it into the pan and cook for 4 minutes, using two spatulas or spoons to toss it with the Chinese leaves over the heat.

4 Add the spring onions, with the salt and pepper and sesame oil. Cook for 1 minute more. Serve at once.

Toasted Noodles with Vegetables

Slightly crisp noodle cakes topped with vegetables make a superb dish.

Serves 4

INGREDIENTS

175 g/6 oz/1½ cups dried
    egg vermicelli
15 ml/1 tbsp vegetable oil
2 garlic cloves, finely chopped
115 g/4 oz/1 cup baby corn cobs
115 g/4 oz/1 cup fresh shiitake
    mushrooms, halved
3 celery sticks, sliced
1 carrot, diagonally sliced
115 g/4 oz/1 cup mangetouts
75 g/3 oz/¾ cup sliced, drained,
    canned bamboo shoots
15 ml/1 tbsp cornflour
15 ml/1 tbsp cold water
15 ml/1 tbsp dark soy sauce
5 ml/1 tsp caster sugar
300 ml/½ pint/1¼ cups vegetable
    stock
salt and ground white pepper
spring onion curls, to garnish

bamboo shoots
baby corn cobs
carrot
celery
shiitake mushrooms
dried egg vermicelli

NUTRITIONAL NOTES
PER PORTION:

ENERGY 316 Kcals/1462 KJ **FAT** 3.8 g
SATURATED FAT 0.4 g
CHOLESTEROL 0 mg

1 Bring a saucepan of water to the boil. Add the egg vermicelli and cook according to instructions on the packet until just tender. Drain, refresh under cold water, drain again, then dry thoroughly on kitchen paper.

2 Heat 2.5 ml/½ tsp oil in a non-stick frying pan or wok. When it starts to smoke, spread half the noodles over the base. Fry for 2–3 minutes until lightly toasted. Carefully turn the noodles over (they stick together like a cake), fry the other side, then slide on to a heated serving plate. Repeat with the remaining noodles to make two cakes. Keep hot.

3 Heat the remaining oil in the clean pan, then fry the garlic for a few seconds. Halve the corn cobs lengthways, add to the pan with the mushrooms, then stir-fry for 3 minutes, adding a little water, if needed, to prevent the mixture burning. Add the celery, carrot, mangetouts and bamboo shoots. Stir-fry for 2 minutes or until the vegetables are tender-crisp.

4 Mix the cornflour to a paste with the water. Add the mixture to the pan with the soy sauce, sugar and stock. Cook, stirring, until the sauce thickens. Season with salt and white pepper. Divide the vegetable mixture between the noodle cakes, garnish with the spring onion curls and serve immediately. Each noodle cake serves two people.

Stir-fried Noodles with Beansprouts

A classic Chinese noodle dish that makes a marvellous accompaniment.

Serves 4

INGREDIENTS
175 g/6 oz/1½ cups dried
    egg noodles
15 ml/1 tbsp vegetable oil
1 garlic clove, finely chopped
1 small onion, halved and sliced
225 g/8 oz/4 cups beansprouts
1 small red pepper, seeded and cut
    into strips
1 small green pepper, seeded and
    cut into strips
2.5 ml/½ tsp salt
1.5 ml/¼ tsp ground white pepper
30 ml/2 tbsp light soy sauce

*dried
egg noodles*

onion

garlic

*soy
sauce*

beansprouts

*red and
green peppers*

NUTRITIONAL NOTES
PER PORTION:

ENERGY 233 Kcals/1122 KJ **FAT** 6.8 g
SATURATED FAT 1.4 g
CHOLESTEROL 13 mg

1 Bring a saucepan of water to the boil. Cook the noodles for 4 minutes until just tender, or according to the instructions on the packet. Drain, refresh under cold water and drain again.

2 Heat the oil in a non-stick frying pan or wok. When the oil is very hot, add the garlic, stir briefly, then add the onion slices. Cook, stirring, for 1 minute, then add the beansprouts and peppers. Stir-fry for 2–3 minutes.

3 Stir in the cooked noodles and toss over the heat, using two spatulas or wooden spoons, for 2–3 minutes or until the ingredients are well mixed and have heated through.

4 Add the salt, pepper and soy sauce and stir thoroughly before serving the noodle mixture in heated bowls.

Singapore Rice Vermicelli

Simple and speedily prepared, this lightly curried rice noodle dish is a full meal in a bowl.

Serves 4

INGREDIENTS
225 g/8 oz/2 cups dried
   rice vermicelli
15 ml/1 tbsp vegetable oil
1 egg, lightly beaten
2 garlic cloves, finely chopped
1 large fresh red or green chilli,
   seeded and finely chopped
15 ml/1 tbsp medium curry powder
1 red pepper, seeded and
   thinly sliced
1 green pepper, seeded and
   thinly sliced
1 carrot, cut into matchsticks
1.5 ml/¼ tsp salt
60 ml/4 tbsp vegetable stock
115 g/4 oz cooked peeled prawns,
   thawed if frozen
75 g/3 oz lean ham, cut into
   1 cm/½ in cubes
15 ml/1 tbsp light soy sauce

vegetable stock

ham   garlic   red and green peppers

soy sauce   curry powder   prawns

egg   carrot   chilli

dried rice vermicelli

1 Soak the rice vermicelli in a bowl of boiling water for 4 minutes, or according to the instructions on the packet, then drain thoroughly and set aside.

2 Heat 5 ml/1 tsp of the oil in a non-stick frying pan or wok. Add the egg and scramble until set. Remove with a slotted spoon and set aside.

NUTRITIONAL NOTES
PER PORTION:

ENERGY 326 Kcals/1500 KJ **FAT** 6.4 g
SATURATED FAT 1.2 g
CHOLESTEROL 152 mg

3 Heat the remaining oil in the clean pan. Stir-fry the garlic and chilli for a few seconds, then stir in the curry powder. Cook for 1 minute, stirring, then stir in the peppers, carrot sticks, salt and stock.

4 Bring to the boil. Add the prawns, ham, scrambled egg, rice vermicelli and soy sauce. Mix well. Cook, stirring, until all the liquid has been absorbed and the mixture is hot. Serve at once.

Seafood Soup Noodles

Audible sounds of enjoyment are a compliment to the Chinese cook, so slurping this superb soup is not only permissible, but positively desirable.

Serves 6

INGREDIENTS

175 g/6 oz tiger prawns, peeled
    and deveined
225 g/8 oz monkfish fillet, cut
    into chunks
225 g/8 oz salmon fillet, cut
    into chunks
5 ml/1 tsp vegetable oil
15 ml/1 tbsp dry white wine
225 g/8 oz/2 cups dried
    egg vermicelli
1.2 litres/2 pints/5 cups fish stock
1 carrot, thinly sliced
225 g/8 oz asparagus, cut into
    5 cm/2 in lengths
30 ml/2 tbsp dark soy sauce
5 ml/1 tsp sesame oil
salt and ground black pepper
2 spring onions, cut into thin rings,
    to garnish

1 Mix the prawns and fish in a bowl. Add the vegetable oil and wine with 1.5 ml/¼ tsp salt and a little pepper. Mix lightly, cover and marinate in a cool place for 15 minutes.

2 Bring a large saucepan of water to the boil and cook the noodles for 4 minutes until just tender, or according to the instructions on the packet. Drain the noodles thoroughly and divide among four serving bowls. Keep hot.

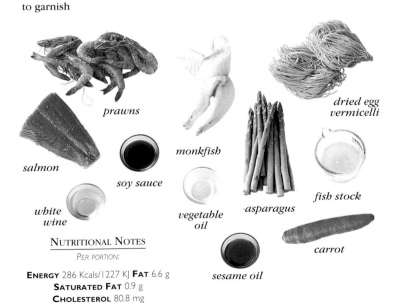

prawns
salmon
soy sauce
monkfish
white wine
vegetable oil
asparagus
dried egg vermicelli
fish stock
carrot
sesame oil

NUTRITIONAL NOTES
PER PORTION:

ENERGY 286 Kcals/1227 KJ **FAT** 6.6 g
SATURATED FAT 0.9 g
CHOLESTEROL 80.8 mg

3 Bring the fish stock to the boil in a separate pan. Add the prawns and monkfish, cook for 1 minute, add the salmon and cook for 2 minutes more.

4 Using a slotted spoon, lift the fish and prawns out of the stock, add to the noodles in the bowls and keep hot.

VARIATION

Try this simple recipe using rice vermicelli for a slightly different texture and taste.

5 Strain the stock through a sieve lined with muslin or cheesecloth into a clean pan. Bring to the boil and cook the carrot and asparagus for 2 minutes, then add the soy sauce and sesame oil, with salt to taste. Stir well.

6 Pour the stock and vegetables over the noodles and seafood, garnish with the spring onions and serve.

Heavenly Jellies with Fruit

Delicate, vanilla-flavoured jelly, set with ribbons of egg white within it, makes a delightful dessert served with fresh fruit.

Serves 6

INGREDIENTS
10 g/¼ oz agar agar
900 ml/1½ pints/3¾ cups boiling
    water
115 g/4 oz/½ cup caster sugar
5 ml/1 tsp vanilla essence
1 egg white, lightly beaten
225 g/8 oz/1½ cups strawberries
450 g/1 lb fresh lychees, or
    475 g/19 oz can lychees, drained

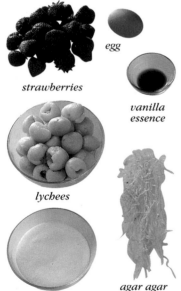

strawberries

egg

*vanilla
essence*

lychees

agar agar

caster sugar

NUTRITIONAL NOTES
PER PORTION:

ENERGY 131 Kcals/560 KJ FAT 0.1 g
SATURATED FAT 0 g
CHOLESTEROL 0 mg

1 Put the agar agar into a saucepan. Add the boiling water, return to the boil and then lower the heat. Simmer the mixture for 10–15 minutes, stirring occasionally, until the agar agar has dissolved completely.

2 Stir in the sugar. As soon as it has dissolved, strain the syrup through a fine sieve placed over a bowl. Return the mixture to the saucepan.

3 Immediately stir in the vanilla essence, then gently pour in the egg white in a steady stream; the heat will cook the egg. Stir once to distribute the threads of cooked egg white.

4 Pour the mixture into a shallow 28 x 18 cm/11 x 7 in baking tray and allow to cool. The jelly will set at room temperature, but will set faster and taste better if it is transferred to the fridge as soon as it has cooled completely.

5 Cut the strawberries in halves or quarters. If using fresh lychees, peel them and remove the stones. Divide the fruit among six small serving dishes or cups.

VARIATION
The jelly can be made with equal amounts of coconut milk and water and served with mangoes for a more tropical taste.

6 Turn the jelly out of the tray and cut it into diamond shapes to serve with the strawberries and lychees.

87

Pears with Ginger and Star Anise

Star anise and ginger give a refreshing twist to these poached pears. Serve them chilled.

Serves 4

INGREDIENTS
75 g/3 oz/6 tbsp caster sugar
300 ml/½ pint/1¼ cups white
   dessert wine
thinly pared rind and juice of
   1 lemon
7.5 cm/3 in piece of fresh root
   ginger, bruised
5 star anise
10 cloves
600 ml/1 pint/2½ cups cold water
6 slightly unripe pears
25 g/1 oz/3 tbsp drained, preserved
   ginger in syrup, sliced
fromage frais, to serve

preserved ginger   *white wine*

star anise   *cloves*

lemon

root ginger

pears

caster sugar

NUTRITIONAL NOTES
PER PORTION:

ENERGY 235 Kcals/1000 KJ **FAT** 0.6 g
SATURATED FAT 1.4 g
CHOLESTEROL 0 mg

1 Place the caster sugar, dessert wine, lemon rind and juice, fresh root ginger, star anise, cloves and water into a saucepan just large enough to hold the pears snugly in an upright position. Bring to the boil.

2 Meanwhile, peel the pears, leaving the stems intact. Add them to the wine mixture, making sure that they are totally immersed in the liquid.

3 Return the wine mixture to the boil, lower the heat, cover and simmer for 15–20 minutes or until the pears are tender. Lift out the pears with a slotted spoon and place them in a heatproof dish. Boil the wine syrup rapidly until it is reduced by about half, then pour over the pears. Allow them to cool, then chill.

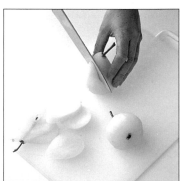

4 Cut the pears into thick slices and arrange these on four serving plates. Remove the ginger and whole spices from the wine sauce, stir in the preserved ginger and spoon the sauce over the pears. Serve with fromage frais.

Golden Steamed Sponge Cake

Cakes are not traditionally served for dessert in China, but this light sponge is very popular with dim sum at lunch time.

Serves 8

INGREDIENTS
175 g/6 oz/1½ cups plain flour
5 ml/1 tsp baking powder
1.5 ml/¼ tsp bicarbonate of soda
3 large eggs
115 g/4 oz/⅔ cup soft light
   brown sugar
45 ml/3 tbsp walnut oil
30 ml/2 tbsp golden syrup
5 ml/1 tsp vanilla essence

brown sugar   *eggs*

golden syrup   *walnut oil*

vanilla essence

plain flour

baking powder

bicarbonate of soda

NUTRITIONAL NOTES
PER PORTION:

ENERGY 213 Kcals/909 KJ **FAT** 6.8 g
SATURATED FAT 1.1 g
CHOLESTEROL 88 mg

1 Sift the flour, baking powder and bicarbonate of soda into a bowl. Line an 18 cm/7 in diameter bamboo steamer, or cake tin with non-stick baking paper.

2 In a mixing bowl, whisk the eggs with the sugar until thick and frothy. Beat in the oil and syrup, then let the mixture stand for about 30 minutes.

3 Add the dry ingredients to the egg mixture with the vanilla essence, beating rapidly to form a thick batter.

4 Pour the batter into the paper-lined steamer or tin. Cover and steam over boiling water for 30 minutes or until the sponge springs back when gently pressed with a finger. Allow to cool for a few minutes before serving.

Pancakes with Red Bean Paste

Sweetened red beans are often used in desserts because the colour is associated with good luck.

Serves 4

INGREDIENTS
600 ml/1 pint/2½ cups cold water
175 g/6 oz/1 scant cup aduki beans, soaked overnight in cold water
115 g/4 oz/1 cup plain flour
1 large egg, lightly beaten
300 ml/½ pint/1¼ cups semi-skimmed milk
5 ml/1 tsp vegetable oil
75 g/3 oz/6 tbsp caster sugar
2.5 ml/½ tsp vanilla essence
fromage frais, to serve (optional)

aduki beans

egg

vegetable oil

vanilla essence

plain flour

semi-skimmed milk

caster sugar

NUTRITIONAL NOTES
PER PORTION:

ENERGY 356 Kcals/1556 KJ **FAT** 4.3 g
SATURATED FAT 1.3 g
CHOLESTEROL 64 mg

COOK'S TIP
Both the pancakes and the bean paste can be made well in advance and kept frozen, ready for thawing, reheating and assembling when needed.

1 Bring the water to the boil in a saucepan. Drain the beans, add them to the pan and boil rapidly for 10 minutes. Skim off any scum from the surface of the liquid, then lower the heat, cover the pan and simmer, stirring occasionally, for 40 minutes or until the beans are soft.

2 Meanwhile, make the pancakes. Sift the flour into a bowl and make a well in the centre. Pour in the egg and half the milk. Beat, gradually drawing in the flour until it has all been incorporated. Beat in the remaining milk to make a smooth batter. Cover; set aside for 30 minutes.

3 Heat a 20 cm/8 in non-stick omelette pan and brush lightly with the vegetable oil. When the oil is hot, pour in a little of the batter, swirling the pan to cover the base thinly.

4 Cook the pancake for 2 minutes until the bottom has browned lightly. Flip the pancake over and cook the second side for about 1 minute, then slide it on to a plate. Make seven more pancakes in the same way. Cover the pancakes with foil and keep hot.

5 When the beans are soft and all the water has been absorbed, tip them into a food processor and process until almost smooth. Add the sugar and vanilla essence and process briefly until the sugar has dissolved.

6 Spread a little of the bean paste on the centre of each pancake and fold them into flat parcels. Place on a baking sheet and cook under a hot grill for a few minutes until crisp and lightly toasted on each side. Serve immediately, on their own or with a little fromage frais.

Tapioca and Taro Pudding

Usually served warm, this is a light and refreshing "soup", popular with children and adults alike.

Serves 4–6

INGREDIENTS

115 g/4 oz/⅔ cup tapioca
1.5 litres/2½ pints/6 cups cold water
225 g/8 oz taro
150 g/5 oz/⅔ cup rock sugar
300 ml/½ pint/1¼ cups coconut
   milk

taro

rock sugar

coconut milk

tapioca

1 Rinse the tapioca, drain well, then put into a bowl with fresh water to cover. Leave to soak for 30 minutes.

2 Drain the tapioca and put it in a saucepan with 900 ml/1½ pints/3¾ cups water. Bring to the boil, lower the heat and simmer for about 6 minutes or until the tapioca is transparent. Drain, refresh under cold water, and drain again.

3 Peel the taro and cut it into diamond-shaped slices, about 1 cm/½ in thick. Pour the remaining water into a saucepan and bring it to the boil. Add the taro and cook for 10–15 minutes or until it is just tender.

4 Using a slotted spoon, lift out half of the taro slices and set them aside. Continue to cook the remaining taro until it is very soft. Tip the taro and cooking liquid into a food processor and process until smooth.

5 Return the taro "soup" to the clean pan; stir in the sugar and simmer, stirring occasionally, until the sugar has dissolved.

6 Stir in the tapioca, reserved taro and coconut milk. Cook for a few minutes. Serve immediately in heated bowls or cool and chill before serving.

COOK'S TIP
Taro is a starchy tuber that tastes rather like a floury potato. If it is difficult to obtain, use sweet potato instead.

NUTRITIONAL NOTES
PER PORTION:

ENERGY 218 Kcals/930 KJ **FAT** 0.2 g
SATURATED FAT 0.1 g
CHOLESTEROL 0 mg

Toffee Apples

All the flavour and texture of this classic Chinese dessert without the fuss and fat of deep-frying.

Serves 6

INGREDIENTS
25 g/1 oz/2 tbsp butter
75 ml/6 tbsp cold water
40 g/1½ oz/6 tbsp plain flour
1 egg
1 dessert apple
5 ml/1 tsp vegetable oil
175 g/6 oz/¾ cup caster sugar
5 ml/1 tsp sesame seeds

apple   *egg*

sesame seeds

plain flour

caster sugar

vegetable oil

NUTRITIONAL NOTES
PER PORTION:

ENERGY 201 Kcals/881 KJ **FAT** 5.6 g
SATURATED FAT 2.7 g
CHOLESTEROL 48 mg

1 Preheat the oven to 200°C/400°F/ Gas 6. Put the butter and water into a small saucepan and bring to the boil. Remove from the heat and add the flour all at once. Stir vigorously until the mixture forms a smooth paste which leaves the sides of the pan clean.

3 Peel and core the apple and cut it into 1 cm/½ in chunks.

2 Cool the choux paste for 5 minutes, then beat in the egg, mixing thoroughly until the mixture is smooth and glossy.

4 Stir the apple into the choux paste and place teaspoonfuls on a dampened non-stick baking sheet. Bake for 20–25 minutes until brown and crisp on the outside, but still soft inside.

5 When the pastries are cooked, heat the oil in a saucepan over a low heat and add the caster sugar. Cook, without stirring, until the sugar has melted and turned golden brown, then sprinkle in the sesame seeds. Remove the pan from the heat.

COOK'S TIP
A slightly unripe banana can be used instead of an apple to ring the changes.

6 Have ready a bowl of iced water. Add the pastries, a few at a time, to the caramel and toss to coat them all over. Remove with a slotted spoon and quickly dip in the iced water to set the caramel; drain well. Serve immediately. If the caramel becomes too thick before all the choux have been coated, re-heat it gently until it liquefies before continuing.

INDEX